MW01617156

What Children Learn from
Their Parents' Marriage

What Children Learn from Their Parents' Marriage

JUDITH P. SIEGEL, PH.D., C.S.W.

HarperCollins*Publishers*

HarperCollins books may be purchased for educational, business, or sales promotional use. For information please write: Special Markets Department, HarperCollins Publishers Inc., 10 East 53rd Street, New York, NY 10022.

FIRST EDITION

Designed by Elliott Beard

Printed on acid-free paper.

Library of Congress Cataloging-in-Publication Data
Siegel, Judith P.
    What children learn from their parents' marriage / Judith P. Siegel.
       p.   cm.
    Includes bibliographical references and index.
    ISBN 0-06-019188-0
    1. Marriage.   2. Communication in marriage.   3. Parental
influences.   4. Intimacy (Psychology)   I. Title.
HQ734.S594   2000
306.81—dc21   99-35044

00 01 02 03 04 ❖/RRD 10 9 8 7 6 5 4 3 2 1

To Lillian and Gerry—the marriage I learned from; and to Morris, Mitchell, and Jenna—the loves of my life.

Contents

Acknowledgments   XI

Introduction:
Your Marriage—Your Child's Blueprint for Intimacy   XIII

1 **How Children Learn from the Marriage**
   "I Wonder What You Will Remember
   When You Are Grown Up"   I

2 **Establishing the Priority of the Marriage**
   "Dad and I Are the Most Important People
   in Each Other's Lives"   18

3 **Teaching the Value of Interdependence**
   "Mom and I Are Always There for Each Other"   44

4 **Instilling the Importance of Mutual Respect**
   "Marrying Your Mom/Dad Was
   the Best Thing I Ever Did"   67

Contents

5 Maintaining Trust in Word and Deed
   *"Partners in a Marriage Try Not
   to Let Each Other Down"*   84

6 Negotiating Differences Constructively
   *"Sometimes We Disagree, but We Always Stick
   with It and Work It Out"*   115

7 Understanding the Long-Term Effects of Conflict
   *"I'll Never Forget the Looks on
   Their Faces When We Fought"*   139

8 Emphasizing the Positives
   *"Laughing Together and Enjoying
   Each Other Are Part of Who We Are"*   165

9 Building a Better Marriage
   "It Is Never Too Late to Try"   180

Notes   199

Bibliography   211

Index   225

The clinical cases presented in this book are composite characters based upon my practice over the years. All names and details have been changed to protect confidentiality.

Acknowledgments

THIS BOOK WAS INSPIRED by a presentation I was invited to make by a colleague and friend, Peggy Herzog. I thank her for helping me to focus again on a subject I had lost sight of. The time and energy that goes into writing a book is enormous, and this project would never have been completed without the full support of my partner, Morris, and the cooperation of my children, Mitchell and Jenna. Monika Polank also deserves my most sincere thanks for keeping the house running while Mom was once again working at the computer.

Although I had written professional books and journal articles, learning to shift gears for this project was quite challenging. Jane Dystel was incredibly helpful in developing the proposal for this book, and I thank her for her patience and ongoing support. I am also deeply indebted to my editor at HarperCollins, Gail Winston. She helped me to stay focused, develop my ideas, and, most important, "find my voice." She is a most dedicated and gifted editor. I would also like to thank my secretary at New York University, Richard Lenert, who magically located all the research articles I could not find, and Dean Tom Meenaghan, who gave his full support to this project.

So many friends have offered encouragement, especially Hannah Fox, Michelle Sacks, Alan Gratch, and Lori Rosenfeld. I also would like to acknowledge the contributions of Denny Jewart, whose clinical wisdom has added to my work throughout the years. Denny, Chapter Five is dedicated to you. I also thank Holly Starkman for adding to the questions from a child's perspective. I am deeply appreciative of the support I have received from my family and would like to thank my sisters—Shelley Fingerhut, Wendy Sokolowski, and especially Debbie Naftolin—who read and critiqued the first draft. My parents, Lillian and Gerry Siegel, have given me ongoing encouragement and I am grateful for their love and pride.

Finally, I would like to thank the hundreds of parents and children I have worked with over the past twenty-five years. You have touched me more deeply than you ever imagined.

Introduction:
Your Marriage—
Your Child's Blueprint
for Intimacy

T WO YEARS AGO a colleague asked me if I would be interested in participating in a community event for parents.
The colloquium would consist of a group of local pediatricians,
child psychologists, educators, and other experts who would
address the topic "What Children Need in the Twenty-first Century." I was asked to speak about the changes we could anticipate
in the home, and, specifically, what children would need from
their parents' marriage.

At first I was somewhat taken aback. For the previous fifteen years my practice, speaking engagements, and publications had been almost exclusively devoted to couples therapy, and in subtle but significant ways I had shifted my perspective away from children. This was a shocking realization, for I was also the mother of two young children and struggling with all the changes that had taken place in my own home after they were born. How odd that I, who had worked with families of troubled children for over ten years, had lost touch with this focus. Of course the parents' marriage affected the children. Of course I could speak on that subject at the community lecture.

That night, several parents stopped to talk to me after my presentation. Their interest and heartfelt thanks were very gratifying. But something else happened two weeks later that had an even greater impact on me. Peter and Catherine called for an appointment and said that they had decided to get help with their marriage after hearing me speak. They brought their beautiful eight-month-old daughter, Amy, with them. After they introduced Amy to me, Catherine said, "It took us five years of clinics and infertility treatments to get Amy. I'm forty-four now, and Amy is our only child. Peter and I want her to be happy, but we fight all the time. Even now she looks at us when we start to shout, and if we keep at it, she starts to cry. Help us for her sake."

I will say more about Peter, Catherine, and Amy later in this book. In fact, the book is filled with families I have known and treated for the past twenty-five years. My first professional job was as a social worker in Toronto's Hospital for Sick Children, where I worked with families whose children had physical symptoms that did not have a medical cause. In this capacity I worked with several hundred parents, all of whom dearly loved their children but who had no idea that the tensions and problems in their marriages were having such a devastating impact on their offspring. This was my first exposure to the extent to which children react to issues that parents incorrectly assume are "private," or are beyond a child's awareness. My years of experience with these families helped me realize the power of the marriage in shaping the personalities and well-being of the children. In fact, I grew increasingly interested in marriages, and chose to pursue this area in my doctoral studies.

Although my interest in marriage therapy was originally based on my respect for the importance of the marriage in building a healthy environment for children, I discovered yet another amazing fact: Even though the adults I worked with did not report unhappy family lives or symptomatic childhoods, the problems that interfered with their happiness were also invariably linked to their own parents' marriages.

In helping couples make sense of their expectations and reactions to each other, I quickly realized the extent to which the marriage the child grows up with influences his own future relationships. Almost all the adults I have counseled in marriage therapy have been profoundly affected by their own parents' relationships. Beliefs about intimacy "learned" in childhood had led to fears, defensive postures, and expectations that worked against intimacy. Even marital partners seemed unconsciously chosen so that aspects of the parents' marriage would be re-created.

I was rather surprised to discover that what to me seemed so obvious was rarely mentioned in the professional literature. Therapists working with individuals emphasized the extent to which children are affected by the relationships they have with each individual parent, but totally neglected the importance of the relationship between the parents. Family therapists focused on the problems that can arise in children when the parents' marriage is conflicted or problematic, but neglected the extent to which the relationship that was observed in childhood profoundly influenced intimacy in the grown child.

The purpose of this book is to create a greater awareness of this dynamic. In my twenty-five years of clinical experience with families of troubled children and with distressed couples, I have come to appreciate that the parents' marriage is critical to the well-being and emotional health of the children. Even if they are barely remembered, these "lessons" of love are very powerful. The marital relationship observed by the child acts like a blueprint upon which all future intimate relationships will be built. For this reason, it is important for parents to step back and examine the lesson plan they have created for their own children. Parents should ask themselves what their children might be noticing and question whether they are helping them create the best possible future.

I am convinced that most parents want the best for their offspring. As I wrote this book, I thought not only about the clients I have worked with over the years, but also about my own two young children. I, like other parents I know, have a wish list for my little ones. I hope that they will grow up knowing how very special they are and will always feel proud of themselves. I hope they will get along with others and know how to compromise when necessary, but I also hope they will know when and how to fight for what is really important to them. Most of all, I hope they will be loved throughout their lives, and that the partners they choose will support them and care for them with the same passion for their well-being as I have.

Parents who want the same kinds of things for their children are active parents. They talk to their kids about things that happen in school or with peers. They think about discipline and self-confidence, and all the things they can do to help their kids develop in healthy ways. However, while most mothers and fathers are deeply invested in the relationship they have with each child, many are unaware of the ways in which the child is affected by the emotional climate of the home. Too often there are problems in the marriage, tensions and unresolved issues that are avoided or postponed indefinitely. Once parents understand the ways in which their children are affected by these issues, I am confident they will find the strength to confront problems and improve their relationship. The outcome has two benefits—a happier home life as well as the hope that this generation of children will be able to learn the positive lessons of love.

When I prepared my lecture for the colloquium two years ago, I realized that while everyone would probably agree that a good marriage provides a solid base for children, most parents need help in realizing the specific components that go into creating a happy home environment. In the chapters that follow, I have identified and discussed seven key ingredients of marriage that provide critical information to children. These are: the priority of the marriage, support, respect, trust, negotiation, conflict resolution, and affection. In determining these themes, I have been guided by theory, by the latest research in child development, and by many years of clinical practice with children and with couples. All of these ideas are translated into the kinds of things that go on between people on a day-to-day basis. I begin the book by explaining how children learn from their parents' marriage. Parents who are interested in psychology may find this theory interesting and informative, but I have written the book in such a way that those who are eager to jump ahead and reading about how each theme affects the children may do so.

Throughout the book, there are two aspects that I would like you to consider. One is the way in which children of all ages react in the "here and now" to the strengths and the problems in their family environment. The second is a look at the consequences that may not be immediately visible during childhood but that later become apparent in the grown child's experience of intimacy. This includes the choice of partner as well as the kinds of problems that they are likely to experience in their own adult relationships.

It is my hope that you will learn more about the ways in which your marriage is affecting your child. Many of you will "see" yourselves in the case examples drawn from my clients. Some chapters will affirm that aspects of your marriage are going well, and you may feel better by recognizing the gift you are giving to your children. Other areas may cause you to look at your situation from a new perspective and question what is going on between you and your partner. I have also provided a list of questions at the end of each chapter to help you focus on your situation and think about specific things your child might be picking up on.

At this point, I would like to share with you the latest aspect of my career development, for I am not only a therapist but also an educator and trainer of therapists. When I teach courses on human development, I am struck by the intense reactions of my older students: men and women who are raising children or whose children are grown. They often shake their heads and with sober self-accusation tell me they wish they had had this information when their children were younger. When I teach courses on marital therapy, students who are engaged, or who have gone through a divorce, tell me how painful it is to look critically at their own relationships and to take responsibility for things they know are their fault. In my classrooms, I can talk to these people, and try to take away the blame and self-condemnation that comes with "knowing." I tell them that in life we all do the best we can at any given moment. The point of understanding relationships from a new perspective is not to blame ourselves but to give us the direction and inspiration to make things better.

I fully realize that this book is both compelling and anxiety-provoking. My friends who are parents were curious but apprehensive when I told them I was writing a book about what children learn from their parents' marriage. The response I got most often was "That's scary," followed quickly by "I'd like to read it when you're finished." Most people worry about doing unintentional harm, and may not want to look too closely at aspects of their own relationships that are difficult to confront. Even parents who are divorced need to think about the relationship they have with their "ex" and the way the children continue to be affected. This book is your classroom. It was not written to make you feel bad, but to give you the information and encouragement you might need to help things turn out for your children the way you really want them to. Because I believe that our own marriages are largely influenced by the marriages we grew up with, I have asked questions to stimulate awareness in this direction as well. This, I know, is also a scary proposition. When I train marriage and family therapists, I often have to help them challenge unconscious beliefs and reactions to their clients. In order to do this, they must think about the relationships they grew up with and the beliefs they hold today. I have discovered that while most find it easy to see the problems in other peoples' lives, it is painful and difficult to look at their own.

In order to fully understand the way your own marriage has developed, it might be useful for you to consider your own parents' marriage and the lessons you inadvertently learned growing up. Once again, I cannot be with you to offer reassurance if doubts or anxieties arise. I can only hope that you will remember that understanding is the first step toward change. By questioning whether your beliefs and expectations have helped you build the life you want, you will be empowered to envision and work toward the kind of relationship you truly desire. This is the beginning of a process that can change the outcome of your marriage and allow all of us to fulfill our greatest obligation—the opportunity to create a positive legacy of love for our children.

1

How Children Learn
from the Marriage

*"I Wonder What You Will Remember
When You Are Grown Up"*

THERE IS AN OLD SAYING that goes "Children do as they see, not as they are told." I'm sure you have heard this before: If you want your child to read more, the best way to accomplish this is to read more yourself. When you want to improve your child's manners or way of dealing with other people, you must first consider how you deal with others and what your child is learning through watching your behavior. Children imitate and become what they observe. While it is true that a child is influenced by the relationship he has with each parent on an individual basis, he also notices and draws conclusions about the relationship between his parents. In fact, that relationship becomes the blueprint for all his future intimate relationships.

I'm Watching You

Children are keen observers of their parents' marriage. Whether or not you are aware of it, your children are noticing the large and the small details of your marital relationship. The truth is, most children are aware of many "private" exchanges their parents assume are beyond their comprehension—a small gesture of comfort, a hostile glance. While your children may not be talking to you about what they are learning, they are drawing conclusions about "what happens" to people who are married. These conclusions will become a permanent part of their beliefs and expectations, and will prepare them to form their own marital relationships when they are older.

Children turn to their parents in order to make sense of the world. They are also highly sensitive and reactive to the emotional climate around them, and are very attuned to conflicts and tensions that do not even directly involve them. Children want to be happy, and do best when their environment is peaceful and secure. In order to avoid being punished or creating a problem, children try to figure out the rules—and then just how far they can bend them.

But psychologists have discovered that children do not need to learn everything from firsthand experience. They learn just as much from watching what happens to other people, and then applying the "rules" to themselves. Psychologist Alfred Bandura was able to demonstrate this in a process that has come to be known as "social learning."[1] Bandura had two groups of children go to a room that contained a variety of toys—including an inflated plastic "Bobo" doll that would sway when punched. The first group of children played freely with all the toys, including Bobo. Before entering the playroom the second group of children were shown a tape in which a child started to play with Bobo and then was sharply reprimanded by an adult who warned the child not to play with the doll anymore. After watching this tape, the children were led to the same toy-filled room. Bandura discovered that the children in his second group played freely with most of the toys, but that not one child would have anything to do with Bobo! Even though they had not been directly instructed to leave Bobo alone, they had learned through watching the tape and seeing what happened to others that it would be safer to choose a different toy.

In the same way, your children are keen observers of your marriage. They pay attention to when and how you disagree, notice how you and your partner react to each other, and in countless ways form impressions about the rules of married life. Some of what they learn has to do with roles, the activities that define what a mommy or a daddy does. You may have pleasant memories or current stories of your child pretending to be a mommy, and acting out the part with enough skill to earn an Emmy. However, children also tune in to the emotional climate and the sense of well-being between family members. Children watch how you and your partner interact and handle situations together. They then draw conclusions about how married people treat each other, for better or for worse.

If Monika watches her parents talk about buying a new car, she learns how married grown-ups work together in making decisions. When they are able to talk calmly and share ideas and different perspectives, Monika learns that both parents are respected, and that differences are okay and safe to express. If Monika's dad acts like his wife's ideas are stupid and that the decision is basically his to make, Monika learns a great deal about power and how people work out their differences. Mom and Dad may not even be aware that Monika has been listening and would probably be startled to realize that Monika's reaction to them as a couple will pave the way to her own beliefs about intimate relationships.

What Do You See?

Do you ever wonder what your children are thinking? Sometimes they amuse us with the explanations they construct. Sometimes they amaze us with their perception and intuition. What children notice, believe, and remember changes as they develop.

What Monika learns about her parents' marriage is partially based on her age, but it is also based on what she has come to expect because of earlier observations of her parents' marriage. Psychologists have learned that children, from a very early age, create a mental road map to help them make sense of the world around them. This is necessary in order to put new situations in a context that makes them understandable so that information can be processed more efficiently. Even as adults, we use what we already know to interpret new events. The underlying structure, which is called a "schema," is occasionally modified to absorb new information, but most of our interpretations and conclusions reflect the belief system that is already in place. Research studies on children and adults have shown that people select or focus on information that will confirm their beliefs, and disregard or minimize evidence to the contrary.[2]

The research of Jean Piaget illustrates this very well.[3] I remember watching a fascinating tape that showed the experiment in which preschool children were shown two beakers that had been placed on a small table. The first beaker, tall and very thin, was filled with water. One at a time, each child watched as the water was poured into the second container, which was short but wide in circumference. When the children were asked "Which vase has more water?," they all agreed that the tall vase held more. Even though they had watched the same amount of water repeatedly being poured from one vase to the other, the children explained that the water level in the first vase was higher, and therefore it had "more." The children had developed a schema of size that showed a grasp of

4

height but not of diameter. Despite the evidence that it was exactly the same amount of water, the schema that "taller means more" led them to draw specific conclusions. The concept of diameter is too sophisticated for young children to grasp. Eventually the children will be able to modify their schemas of dimension, but even then their first instinct will be to expect height to predict size. The original beliefs stay with us and continue to influence our thinking for many years.

But how do children learn about relationships? While psychologists know a great deal about how children learn right from wrong in their friendships and in social situations, there is very little research on how children make sense of family relationships. One of the few studies I have come across on this area was a research project about stepfamilies.[4] Although this was not the main purpose of the study, by talking with children, psychologist Ann Bernstein noticed that children of different ages define "family" quite differently. Preschool children are self-centered, and think mainly about which adults provide caretaking for them. School-age children are more factual, and define the family according to history and living arrangements. Adolescents, who have developed the capacity to think abstractly, use more complex concepts such as reciprocity and the nature of the relationship between parent and child. Children slowly develop the ability to understand things in a multidimensional way. Thus, her parents' discussion about a new car will be understood and reacted to differently depending on whether Monika is five or fifteen. Children who are young are more vulnerable to blaming themselves when their parents quarrel; older children can allow that their parents have a relationship that does not directly involve them. The final product or schema of the parents' marriage probably contains elements from all of the developmental phases.

How Accurate Can This Be?

The child's schema is based on the observed relationship, but it is very much a belief that is constructed by the child, and open to the child's interpretations and emotional reactions. The schema consists of memories, but it is much more than the sum of the memories it holds. In fact, memories have been found to be extremely inconsistent, while schemas persist. For example, psychologists have studied how frequently people embellish or change, without any awareness of this, the details of major events from the past.[5] In one study, college students were asked how they learned that the space shuttle *Challenger* had exploded. When they were asked the same question several years later, their answers had changed dramatically. None the less, all swore that their most recent answers were true, and were shocked to read their earlier responses. However, when adults were asked different questions about their parents' marriage and then given the same questionnaire four years later, their answers were almost identical. Time had not altered their evaluations. Unlike memories of single events, the schema of a parents' marriage is persistent, almost, as some have suggested, a part of our identity.[6]

But it is never too late to change the marital blueprint that we are handing to our children. Even though our children have witnessed things that we may regret, adult children are able to discriminate between different phases of their family during the time they were growing up. Studies have shown that adults can describe the differences between their parents' early marriage and the way things were years later.[7] Somehow, multiple aspects become integrated to create an overall schema.

It should also be emphasized that the child actively constructs this inner picture. Each child is sensitive or receptive to different issues, and experiences family events in a unique manner.[8] If you want to test this idea, ask your brothers and sisters questions about various aspects of your childhood family. Even though you all come from the same family, each sibling will evaluate their family life quite differently and will come up with their own "private reality." While you may agree about the number of bedrooms in your childhood home, there will probably be a wide variety of responses to questions about family humor, or decision making. So rather than search for "the truth" of what happened, it is more important to accept the subjective realities that were produced.

Silent Beliefs

People rarely stop to question what they believe to be true and how they have come to these conclusions. Schema are not fully recognizable, and often operate in silent ways. After a schema has been formed, it usually becomes "tacit" knowledge—that is, a belief that is accepted as being universally true. These kinds of beliefs lead us to assume that what worked for us is true for everyone. For example, a child who grows up in a typical American family would notice that people eat with forks and knives. He would probably take this for granted, and would assume that everyone eats this way. Imagine his surprise when he is first taken to a Chinese restaurant and discovers that people also eat with chopsticks! Perhaps he has been exposed to European friends or relatives who hold their forks in the same hand throughout a meal. Before the chopstick experience, the child may not have noticed this. The schema of how people eat may not have been sufficiently jolted to register the more subtle differences. However, once the child has acknowledged that people eat in different ways, he may be more attuned to noticing the variations that exist.

Much of what children observe about their parents' marriage becomes "tacit" information, beliefs that are apparent only through the way in which events are interpreted and reacted to. However, the beliefs of what marriage should be like can be traced to what a person was exposed to in his childhood family. Frequently, partners are surprised when they compare their backgrounds and discover just how different two families can be. Each spouse is convinced that the way things were done in their own family is the "right" way. I once worked with a couple who, after ten years, continued to fight about the "right" thing to serve for Thanksgiving dinner!

What needs to be emphasized is the power of these early beliefs. The tacit knowledge that is absorbed in childhood forms the beliefs that help explain how culture is passed from one generation to another. Even when a person is exposed to a different environment in adulthood, he or she continues to hold on to the beliefs, values, and expectations acquired in the childhood home.[9]

I Am My Mother's Daughter; I Am My Father's Son

Another way of understanding how your child is affected by your marriage is through the psychological process of identification— the way she models herself after those adults who are important in her day-to-day life. It is easy to notice when your child is imitating you or your partner by "borrowing" a way of speaking, a mannerism, or a way of walking. But unlike role-playing, identifications are not temporary imitations that are abandoned as the child moves on to the next play event. Initially, identifications are borrowed, but they eventually become characteristics or attributes that the child experiences as part of herself. Whenever a part of the child's psyche becomes "like" a parent, the process of identification is at work.[10]

It is misleading to think that children identify only with the same-sex parent. Children are not fully aware of sexual differences and their own sexual identity until the age of three or four. Until that time, they freely model both parents. Even after that time, they may continue to identify with aspects of both parents, although the way they view the same-sex parent definitely has a role in shaping identity.[11]

Children do not necessarily like all the characteristics of their parents, and do not always accept the role models they have been given. This becomes more evident as children get older and attempt to distinguish themselves from their parents by becoming more like their peers, media stars, or sports heroes. One way to think about this is as a process called "disidentification," which is the part of identity that is built from a dislike of certain aspects of a parent, and the intent to *not* be like that parent.[12] People can decide to disown certain characteristics, and "do battle" with these identifications. However, even the aspects that have been rejected become part of the person's identity and will remain a source of emotional vulnerability. As psychologist Ruthellen Josselson says, "We are as closely tied to people when we cannot bear finding them in ourselves as when that is what we most wish to do."[13]

What this means is that as your children notice how you interact with your partner, they absorb or adopt certain aspects of each of you within their own identities. If your child feels proud or positive about any given characteristic, it is likely to produce a positive identification. He will "own" that part of you, and will be strongly motivated to become that way in his own marriage. However, when your child feels disgusted or ashamed about how the two of you are behaving, he may try to disidentify with your behavior. Even at an early age, a child can vow to never do or tolerate something he has witnessed in his parents' marriage. A negative identification may cause your child to take a defensive posture when he is older in order to avoid becoming too similar or repeating something he has found to be offensive (for example, a daughter who believes that her mother is selfish because she spends little time with her children yet is constantly socializing may vow to devote herself to taking better care of her own children; a son who watches his father gamble away the rent money may become determined to financially provide for those he loves). This applies to values and ways of treating other family members as well as individual characteristics.[14]

In this way, identification can serve as a source of strength or of tension. Positive identifications can inspire us as we draw upon the parts of ourselves that are most connected to the strengths of our parents. Negative identifications can create overreactions and tension, especially when we find ourselves in situations that awaken the parts of ourselves that have been disavowed.

The Internalized Couple

Within each of us there is a model of marriage based on our early family experiences. The problem is that much of this was formed when we were too young to fully comprehend what marriage is really all about. Our beliefs and expectations are also colored by the emotional world of a child, a world, psychiatrists Jill and David Scharff point out, that is ruled by both fact and fantasy. Our beliefs are certainly based on what we have observed, but there are "extra" qualities inspired by imagination.[15] The outline is drawn from real events, but it is colored in in ways that capture the child's mood and emotional state.

For example, if Monika's father has a loud voice that frightens her, or if he frequently loses control of his anger in angry spats with her mother, Monika's internal couple might be emotionally tinged with terror. She may fantasize that her parents' fights will lead to rage and perhaps to murder. The fantasy image is exaggerated beyond the "facts," but nonetheless it becomes part of the belief system that will influence Monika's own expectations and reactions to conflict.

The internal couple is not a "fact" that the child turns to at will but an emotional reference that has its own ability to influence. Any situation is capable of triggering the beliefs and emotional responses held within this internalized couple. If Monika's reference of marriage is one that is not able to handle conflict safely, she will believe that disagreement may lead to violence and destruction. Her fears and emotional reactions will stay with her for a long time and will complicate her ability to form a trusting, intimate relationship of her own.

When a child's identity holds pockets that are filled with confusion and tension, he may not always exhibit symptoms that indicate that there is a serious problem. Some children show signs of trouble by imitating or acting out these conflicts with their peers. However, for other children, there are no visible signs of problems in childhood. Perhaps the child is overweight; perhaps the child is shy or mistrustful. The consequences of the internalization are not fully appreciated until the child reaches young adulthood and draws on these aspects of his identity to form his own intimate relationship. For reasons that are not entirely understood, we all seem to need to repeat the vulnerabilities and tensions of our childhoods. As adults, we repeat issues that trouble us much in the same way that children try to solve their problems—by doing it over and over again.[16]

In play, children can repeat the same theme endlessly, always searching for a better outcome. What I have learned from my experience as a marriage therapist is that the unfinished business that gets repeated in such painful ways is not always connected to the relationship each individual had with his parents individually. Very often, I am working with painful issues that my clients, as children, internalized from their parents' marriage.

Troubled Children

Children are acutely sensitive to the unresolved conflicts between their parents, and learn that by acting in a certain way they can prevent a conflict from surfacing and threatening the family as a whole. The ways in which children react to tensions between their parents is one of the most important discoveries of family therapy. It is amazing to realize the extent to which children adapt their behavior and personalities to fill a need in their family or to keep the family together.[17] Usually, the parents are the last to recognize this.

When Monika hears her parents fight over which car to buy, she will probably do her very best to break up the fight. Children are uncomfortable and frightened when their parents are in emotional disequilibrium, and instinctively do what they can to restore family peace. Monika might directly appeal to her parents to stop fighting. If this fails, Monika may attempt to distract her parents by making a mess or by fighting with her younger brother. When Monika is being disruptive, her parents must stop their quarrel in order to handle the chaos between the kids. A new role for Monika has been created.

One of the first lessons I learned as a family therapist was the Jekyll/Hyde aspect of many children. A child would be one way when I talked to him privately and completely different when the rest of the family joined the session. Monika's aggressive behavior, which in this example was necessary to prevent her parents' fights, might exist only within the family context. At school, and with friends, Monika might be a sociable, playful little girl. This would be an example of a child who knows how and when to act in ways that resolve the family tensions, but who can establish a genuine self in other situations. However, in other instances, the child's need to fill a particular role for the family causes her to seal off her true self and "become" the person who was needed for the emotional survival of the family. Should this happen to Monika, her sense of herself as disruptive and as the family's problem child would ensure that this side of her becomes known in all spheres of her life.

Examples of the ways in which children behave and develop in relation to family problems have been especially well described in the literature of the children of alcoholic families. In these families, children take on predictable roles, so that one may become super responsible while another becomes the clown or the problem child. The problem child may act out in a serious enough way to bring the entire family to therapy. However, all of the children have the same underlying issues and are vulnerable because of what they learned from their parents' marriage.[18] It is hard for parents to comprehend that a child who is super responsible, or "perfect," may in fact be very troubled and confused. All too often these emotional issues stay submerged until the child is almost grown, and begins to date. Once again, it is not surprising that these young adults are attracted to partners who struggle with similar issues, and that they repeat the dynamics they were exposed to in their childhood home.

Conflict is not the only area that can create problems for children. In some families, there are high levels of anxiety that interfere with the psychological development of the children. Most often this anxiety is related to fears of being abandoned or left alone, which causes people to attach themselves to others in unhealthy ways and become enmeshed. In this kind of family, people are likely to avoid differences and conflict for fear that it might lead to a rupture in closeness. Because anger cannot be tolerated, children stuff their feelings down in ways that lead to psychosomatic and emotional problems. Children who are raised in a climate of underlying anxiety often become insecure and seek excessive closeness to adults in order to feel safe. Because the parents' needs for connection are being met through attachment to their children, they are less likely to support their children's efforts to become independent or socially connected to peers or others outside the family. Thus the undercurrent of anxiety is passed from generation to generation, creating problems in the ways children and their parents experience relatedness to family and to "others."[19]

Children are affected not only by stressful or troubling interactions but by the good as well. When parents are able to show each other respect and affection and work through their differences constructively, they are giving a great deal to their children. Their kids are being provided with a secure environment in which they can focus on their own issues and not take on the burdens of their parents. Children from these families have excellent role models, but more important, they are creating an inner schema of marriage that is filled with positive beliefs and expectations. For them, marriage is a place where people take care of each other, enjoy being with each other, and know how to work out problems.

In contrast, children who come from homes where there is marital discord have a very different experience. They are robbed of their chance to choose their own priorities and become saddled with unfair responsibilities. Their exposure to parents who do not support each other or act in loving ways leads them to believe that marriage is neither safe nor comfortable, and leaves them with doubts about whether people can truly be trusted. When they watch one parent demean, humiliate, or abuse the other, they are put in a conflicted position where neither parent can be identified with in a positive way. Demands for loyalty create pressure and resentment in their daily lives, which makes them dread being put in a similar position as an adult. It is not enough that these children struggle with self-esteem, depression, and intense anger as youngsters; it can be predicted that they will have relationship problems in adulthood.

Issues that were "hot buttons" in the home of one generation will become target areas of emotional reactivity in the next. When parents react to each other in extreme ways, they are usually reexperiencing issues that were problematic in their own childhoods. Children are likely to pick up the emotional upset and develop a vulnerability in the same area. For example, parents who are critical of each other, or who easily blame each other when things go wrong, probably grew up in families that were judgmental and/or demanding. Regardless of whether they confine this way of relating to their marriage or are similarly demanding and critical of their children, they have exposed their kids to a picture of marriage that excludes forgiveness and support. Being judged and blamed are likely to become trigger areas for their children.

Difficulties for children can also develop when the problems between the parents pass from the confines of the marital relationship into the relationship each parent has with the child. Often, parents who are distressed by a characteristic in their partner, but cannot fight directly, take out their frustration on a child who in some way resembles or comes to represent their grievance. In other situations, a child can be looped into the marriage by being pressured into representing one parent's conflict against the other. When a child is used to manage or divert tension from the marriage, a triangle is created. For example, a child may be triangulated into the marriage by a parent who needs support or "parenting" when there are marital problems or unhappiness. In all of these situations, children are exposed to information that distracts them from the priorities of childhood and places overwhelming burdens on them. Once again, while some children develop immediate symptoms, others may appear to be well adjusted until it is time for them to form their own adult intimate relationships.

The Good as Well as the Bad

Since therapists are called when people are in trouble, we tend to use examples of problem situations to illustrate our theories. However, there are many positive lessons of love that children take from their parents' marriage and pass along to their own children. Just as children sense tension and conflict, so do they observe caring and support. Couples who have successful marriages have much to tell us about the secrets to their happiness. Not surprisingly, the positive example of their parents' marriage is often high on their list. When couples speak about a good marriage and how important marriage is to them, they usually acknowledge their own parents' marriage as a positive influence and a source of inspiration.[20]

When children are raised in loving, nurturing environments where parents clearly enjoy each other, they develop an appreciation and a desire for intimacy. Because they have grown up watching and experiencing the comfort and support that comes from intimacy, they are more ready to create it in their own lives. The belief in the goodness of marriage is established in childhood and adolescence, and is already formed by young adulthood. Psychologists who have studied the positive expectation and desire for intimacy have found that men and women who possess this belief are happier in their marriages, enjoy parenting more, and are physically healthier, too.[21] While many factors combine to produce a happy marriage, young adults who value intimacy and expect to have a successful relationship are more likely to achieve it.

Although your children are exposed to many different kinds of marriages as they spend time with their friends' families and get to know the TV families of prime time, the marriage of the nuclear family continues to have a lifelong influence. The actions and values that color your marriage filter into your child's core belief system. Even though the lessons of love are seldom articulated, a child "knows" what to expect based on what he saw going on between you and your partner. The power of this kind of learning cannot be underestimated, especially because it operates in silent ways.

In the following chapters, I will introduce you to people I have worked with who illustrate how and what children learn from their parents' marriage. Most of these people demonstrate the kinds of problems that can develop, either by children who are keeping a fragile peace in the best way they know how or by adults who have traced the connection between their current problems and their parents' marriage. Therapy became a way to recognize and ultimately challenge these problems. However, prevention is a therapist's ultimate goal. By looking at each of these themes in your own marriage, there is hope that your children can learn the positive lessons of love.

2

Establishing the Priority
of the Marriage

*"Dad and I Are the Most Important
People in Each Other's Lives"*

MY CLINICAL WORK with troubled children and unhappy marriages has convinced me that a strong marriage is the foundation of a family's well-being. When parents are in a relationship that provides them with support and affection, they are enriched and nourished so that they can better enjoy themselves and their children. Children who grow up in this atmosphere receive two invaluable gifts: a more stable and consistent family environment, and a blueprint of a happy marriage that will lead them to search for the same when they are older. But the statistics confirm that not enough marriages are working out well. The divorce rate in our country has reached 50 percent and continues to rise. Marriage therapists report a high incidence of unhappy marriages that do not end in divorce but are not responsive to traditional approaches to therapy. Even studies on individuals who are depressed show that half of the people who seek help say that their number one problem is their love relationship.[1] It makes sense, then, to look at what goes on in happy versus unhappy marriages. For it is not only the therapists who notice what is going right or wrong—it is also the children.

One element that I have found to be extremely important in building a solid marriage is the partners' ability to keep the marriage a priority in their lives.[2] For some couples, the challenge comes when they first make a commitment to each other. Even at this early juncture, they are not able to find the right balance between the demands of their partner and their loyalty to their childhood family. For other couples, the difficulty arises later, when children enter their lives and they have to learn how to become parents while making sure that they have privacy and time for their own relationship. In today's hectic, overscheduled world, almost every couple needs help in learning to protect their marriage from the pressures of the outside world.

If parents succumb to the demands of others to the extent that there is too little energy or time left for the marriage, they lose touch with how much they need and value each other, and often find themselves expressing their loss through anger or depression. Even though the marriage is not the only commitment people make in life, it must be treated in a special way if it is to be sustained. When spouses act as if they are more strongly connected to their parents, their children, or their jobs, then the marriage is in trouble. Many individuals I have treated in marital therapy complain of being taken for granted. When I first meet a couple, I usually ask them about the time they spend alone and where the marriage fits among their other commitments and obligations. I have found that a couple who rarely spend time together are not able to support and take care of each other, and that there are painful consequences.

There is a certain atmosphere and culture that is created in each family. The ways in which parents speak to each other, touch each other, talk about each other; the tone that accompanies the minutiae of everyday interactions . . . all lead to the beliefs, values, and expectations that family members share. It is the atmosphere and way of conducting everyday living that is imprinted on the child's schema of a couple. When parents value each other, are happy to see each other, and keep each other's needs in focus, their children learn the importance of marital closeness. When spouses spend little time together and ignore their marriage, they convey to their children that other people and responsibilities are more important. Without intending to, they teach their children that spouses do not necessarily enjoy each other, and that work, extended family, and friends are the real sources of adult gratification and contentment.

"Are You Married to Me or to Your Family?"

Therapists who work with couples and families believe that the family goes through predictable stages of family connectedness.[3] For example, while it is normal for children to love and be attached to their parents, there comes a time when the adolescent must make a shift away from his parents and develop relationships with other adolescents who become equally important. Through the process of emotionally separating from their parents, young people learn how to make room for new people to love.

Learning to establish an intimate relationship with one person is not simple or automatic. Most people struggle to find a balance between self and other, and learn how to work with the differences and disappointments that arise. As the relationship becomes more serious, the willingness to become vulnerable and depend on another person becomes part of the formula for success. But the ability of a relationship to grow and endure is also affected by the way in which each partner can learn to juggle and redefine the responsibilities and commitments they have to their new lover versus their family of childhood.

In order to become a good partner, three distinct identities have to become merged and balanced: the self that is an independent person, the self that is now one half of a couple, and the self that is still a child and a sibling. It is not easy to live up to our own family's expectations while at the same time demonstrating our loyalties to our partner and new extended family. For most people, these challenges peak shortly after the engagement is announced. Planning the wedding is often a stressful experience, where each decision initiates a family battle. At a time that should be blissfully happy, most couples find themselves struggling to balance family members' different expectations and soothe ruffled feathers. For many, the first year of marriage continues to be a stressful time as loyalties, responsibilities, and commitments are repeatedly tested.

When the Extended Family Comes First: Enmeshed Families

While it is true that if you examined how married individuals from different cultures relate to their childhood families you would discover a wide range of options, each has consequences for the marital relationship. In societies where there is more emphasis placed on the group or the family, there is less expectation that the marriage will provide intimacy. Lifelong parent-child ties and loyalty to the family of origin may be expected and viewed as the norm. But in these cultures, there is less emphasis on the importance of love or personal happiness. Adults turn to same-sex friends, extended family, and even children for companionship, stimulation, and connection.[4]

However, in our society, there is a belief that people will find and marry their soul mate. One person is regarded as the ultimate source of friendship and affection, and marriage is viewed as the culmination of romantic love. Because the parts of the marriage that involve romance, sex, and intimacy are designed for a twosome, there is little room for parents or parents-in-law.

But there is more to life than marriage, and each partner must find a way to maintain a comfortable connection to his or her own family. It is rare that both partners have the same perspective and expectations regarding what is the "right" level of involvement. In my own life, I worried about what it meant that my husband saw his mother so infrequently, while he agonized over the time and money I spent on long-distance phone calls with my parents and sisters. Each of us had to work through our different perspectives on what information could be shared and what needed to be kept private within the marriage.

If a couple is not able to create comfortable boundaries with their own families of origin before their children are born, then the situation usually becomes much worse. Parents who have difficulty in letting go of their adult children often find their true calling when the first grandchild is born. A couple that has not learned how to regulate their relationship with the older generation is at a serious disadvantage when confronted with the inevitable deluge of well-intended advice and demands for involvement. Unless these boundaries are clearly defined in the early years of the relationship, the children will learn that their parents value their relationships with members of the extended family above the marriage. This is problematic because it is critical for children to see how important their parents are to each other.

Children who grow up in a home where the extended family is a wedge between their parents may assume that primary loyalty to one's parents or siblings is normal and that parents do not come first in each other's lives. In the most extreme case, one parent's family is deemed special, while the other extended family is devalued. If a parent is more devoted to his family than to his spouse, an insider/outsider perspective may be established, which creates tensions and loyalty issues for the children. The children may be accepted as part of the "superior" family, while their other parent and extended family is cast aside. The children may also grow up with similar prejudices toward others. This kind of superiority often breeds entitlement, which adds additional stress to a relationship. Such was the case for Paul and Irene.

PAUL AND IRENE

Irene met Paul during her first month of college, and was thrilled when eight months later he gave her a diamond ring. When Irene's family met Paul, they described him as "a little rough around the edges, but good potential," and although they gave their approval to the relationship, they made it clear to Paul that he needed to spruce up his manners and wardrobe in order to fit into their family. Irene's mother was very sensitive to other people's judgments and had always made sure that her family made a positive impression wherever they went. She had married a man who was financially successful but whose parents had been poor immigrants. Although she was courteous to her in-laws, the only close family connection that was encouraged was to her own family of childhood. Irene and her two brothers were close to the relatives on their mother's side of the family but were almost strangers to their father's extended family.

Now the cycle was being perpetuated, with Irene's family the successful, socially appropriate one, and with Paul being viewed as the son of working-class people. Despite Paul's intelligence, wonderful sense of humor, and charm, he was regarded by Irene's family as "less than." Paul had learned about his future mother-in-law's description of him, and was wounded by her comments. "Just as long as you don't think that, we're okay," he had told his bride to be. But as the wedding got closer and closer, the extent of the problem became more obvious.

Irene's parents suggested that the couple take the large amount of money designated for Irene's wedding and use it as a down payment on a home. There would still be a small reception, but only for immediate relatives and close friends. Paul, however, came from a very large family that valued celebration. His parents were hurt and confused when they learned of the couple's option, and suggested that the wedding gifts they received would help them buy a home. In their eyes, there was no rush for a home, but every reason to celebrate the first wedding of Paul's generation in their family. Paul also wondered if Irene's mother was ashamed of his family and afraid of what her friends would think when they saw how poor and unsophisticated they were. When Irene supported her parents' offer, Paul was surprised and hurt. After realizing the extent to which Irene was influenced by her family and unresponsive to his feelings, he called off the wedding.

Problems for the Children

While there are enough successful examples of close relationships with parents and in-laws to warn us against judging parent–grown child involvement as "wrong," there is also evidence that parents who are overly connected to their own parents may be complicating the lives of their children. There are a number of family therapists who have drawn connections between interfamily closeness and problems with children and adolescents. Several psychiatrists have found that adolescents with severe anorexia come from families where there is excessive overinvolvement between the mother and her childhood family.[5] Jill Harkaway, who works with obese children, similarly notes that the majority of her patients come from families where the parents have not been successful in forming an independent identity and separating from their own parents.[6] These kinds of families are described by family therapists as being "enmeshed," and, most often, one or both parents are aligned with their own parents instead of with their spouse. The pattern of cross-generational ties is likely to be perpetuated, creating stress and emotional burdens for the children. This was quite evident in a family I worked with a few years ago.

THE PERLMUTTER FAMILY

Rhonda and Jack Perlmutter had been in marital therapy once before, but had dropped out after a few sessions. They were sarcastic and deprecating in their description of their previous therapist, whom they viewed as naive and superficial, and had doubts that I could be of any help to them either. But the children's pediatrician was concerned about the family environment, and had urged the couple to seek help once more.

The couple had three grown children and one preschool-age daughter. Within the first few minutes, I could see that the youngest child was an important part of the couple's current problems but that this marriage had been in trouble before she was born. Elana had been adopted when Rhonda was forty-six, one year after the youngest natural child left for college. While Jack was pleased about his opportunities to travel more and enjoy hunting, a sport he was passionately invested in, Rhonda's loneliness was unbearable to her, and she pushed until Jack agreed to the adoption. Now Rhonda felt overwhelmed with a very active child and a husband who was unwilling to change his lifestyle. He worked long hours, and left home early each weekend morning to enjoy the best hours of hunting. When Rhonda looked to me for support, Jack snarled, "What did you expect? I told you before you adopted her that I was not going to change my work habits or give up hunting. This was our bargain. You agreed to it, and now you're stuck with it!"

Once the conflict had been introduced in the session, the hostility between the partners erupted full force. Within seconds they were screaming at each other and hurling insults. It took all of my strength to calm them down enough to learn a little about them as individuals, and their life before their youngest daughter had joined the family.

Rhonda was the youngest of three children born to parents who had emigrated through political asylum. Although her parents were hardworking, loving people, they never recovered from political oppression and were always fearful and suspicious of outsiders. Their need to protect their children was exacerbated when Rhonda and her brother developed chronic asthma within one year of each other. Because Rhonda's mother believed that the children were fragile and could die if exposed to another illness, all three children were kept at home and tutored for several years. Even after they were able to go back to school, Rhonda's mother disapproved of Rhonda's making friends or developing outside interests. "You have me and the family—what could you possibly want from someone else who doesn't even care about you?"

Rhonda joked that in some ways it was a miracle that she ever got married. The relationship between her mother and the three children was so tight that there was no room for outsiders. Even when the children were teenagers, they seldom dated or participated in interests outside the family. But Rhonda had always yearned for children of her own, and secretly started to date Jack when she was twenty years old. In her mind, Jack could be "adopted" into their family unit, eventually allowing her to fulfill her mother's greatest wish—to become a grandmother.

Jack was also somewhat of a loner, and had dated few women before he met Rhonda. Born to a family who valued academic success, Jack had floundered in school due to undiagnosed dyslexia. His difficulty in learning to read was a source of embarrassment to him and his parents, and he suffered intense feelings of failure. One problem seemed to lead to another, and Jack's nerves caused him to stutter at school, a condition that prompted the other children to tease and avoid him. As a result, Jack turned to hunting—a sport that gave him a chance to excel and find peace in an environment where he was totally in control. Eventually, Jack's learning problem was detected and corrected. As if to compensate for his earlier failure, Jack went on to excel in graduate school, and to create a demanding consulting business that was highly respected.

Jack and Rhonda had been fixed up by a mutual friend. Even though Jack was doing well in his business, he had never acquired casual social skills, and was attracted to Rhonda's exuberance and "chatty" style. Rhonda knew that her parents would approve of Jack's financial success and his quiet nature, and was thrilled to have a chance to establish a family of her own. Even though Jack knew that Rhonda was deeply involved with her mother and sister, he thought that these relationships would keep Rhonda busy so that he could pursue his business demands and continue to hunt. When the children were born, Rhonda's family helped out to keep this pattern going.

But over the years, the couple had become critical of and dissatisfied with each other. Jack preferred to have quiet time at home to unwind, and resented what he described as Rhonda's constant need to talk. Rhonda often felt alone and overwhelmed, and did not know how to handle the anxiety that surfaced as her children became ill with normal infections or started to have sleepovers at their friends' homes. Things grew worse when Rhonda's mother died unexpectedly. Her sister was involved with her own husband and baby, and for the first time, Rhonda felt utterly alone. Her anxiety led her to overeat, which Jack responded to with contempt. The marriage was falling apart, and the older kids were miles away.

When they were younger, each of the children had taken a turn being Mom's confidant and best friend. While Jack had allowed these close relationships to develop, he had compensated by making sure that the children were active in sports and had musical

27

interests, and went to sleep-away camps each summer. Now the children were young adults, making lives for themselves far from their parents' home. But their absences created a crisis for Rhonda. Without her mother, she was alone and vulnerable. She had never truly developed a relationship with her husband, and looked to the mother-child relationship to provide her with identity and connection. Her need to adopt a new baby to fill the void left by the older children bordered on desperation—for she knew no other way to exist.

When I met the youngest daughter, I could see why Rhonda felt like she had her hands full. Elana was a whirlwind of action and commotion, a child always on the go. Rhonda said that Elana had recently been diagnosed with ADD, but both parents were skeptical that medication was the best plan for such a young child, and suspicious of the accuracy of the testing process. Both Rhonda and Jack could see that their marital situation added to Elana's behavior, as she was almost uncontrollable when her parents started to fight. Within minutes, Elana would break something or call for help, forcing Rhonda to focus all of her attention on her youngest child. While Rhonda got some satisfaction from being needed, she would also become exhausted and frustrated. Her dream of having a darling daughter to play with was shattered by the demands of a child who added to her anxiety and self-doubt. However, the prescription of an invested, anxious mother devoted to a closely attached daughter was firmly in place. As long as the marriage remained caustic, this formula was unlikely to ever change.

Unfortunately, I could not help this couple get past their rather rigid positions. Rhonda continued to blame Jack for making her life miserable, and Jack refused to compromise his lifestyle. For Jack, happiness came from work, sports, and telephone contact with his elder children. Rhonda became increasingly connected to Elana and a small group of professionals who could help her manage her day-to-day challenges.

Who Comes First?

Rhonda and Jack are not the only partners who have stopped turning to each other to get their needs met. For many, the disappointments and stressful process of having to negotiate to get one's needs met become turnoffs that make it seem easier to turn elsewhere. Perhaps the expectations placed on contemporary marriage are too excessive, as partners look to each other to provide friendship, terrific sex, and all the emotional ingredients that create what most of us think of as intimacy. Ruthellen Josselson, who has made important contributions to the field, suggests that intimacy cannot be attained unless a person feels valued, wanted, and cared for.[7] There are times when it is easy to respond to a partner's needs, but there are also times when what is being asked for is just too demanding. Too often partners have simultaneous or competing needs, but think that their own situation is more important and should be responded to first. Intimacy often requires patience, self-sacrifice, and the ability to juggle resources so that both partners can be accommodated.

In my experience, this is one of the explanations for so many marriages turning sour or angry. In our grandparents' era, commitment to the family's overall well-being was the priority, and the paths men and women had to take to contribute to family success were clearly defined. Fewer demands were put on the marital relationship, and there were almost no alternatives aside from working harder to make things better. Today there is a greater emphasis on each individual's right to happiness and fulfillment. Women as well as men invest in work and social and athletic pursuits that provide stimulation and gratification. As a result, a person who has developed other sources of personal fulfillment will have a very different reaction to the demands that accompany intimacy than will a person who regards marriage as the most fulfilling aspect of life.[8] For the latter, decisions that prioritize the marriage or partner rather than the self are not necessarily experienced as sacrifice, as the rewards that come from a happy marriage are the most important. But if a person believes that success at work is the way to achieve happiness, then time and energy devoted to the marriage may seem like an interference or an unfulfilling obligation. When parents value their marital relationship, they make decisions that respect not only the partner but the marriage itself. When this happens, there is less conflict between what is good for "me" and what is good for "us."

When Work Comes First: Workaholic Families

The idea of making the marriage a priority may sound appealing to many parents, but in order to make this happen, the realities of work must be considered. Parents may be wedded to their jobs for different reasons. It is often difficult for today's families to re-create the lifestyle they grew up with. The cost of housing and other related living expenses have soared, while incomes have increased at a much more modest rate. In an era of layoffs and corporate mergers, workers experience more demands on their time. In order to keep their jobs, many adults find that they are routinely putting in ten- to twelve-hour days.

While it is true that the majority of mothers work, most married women balance work with family responsibilities, and do not regard themselves as the family's primary wage earner. Because men typically earn more than women and because it is less threatening to the status quo, most couples define the husband as being primarily responsible for the family's financial security. Psychologist Gill Barnes suggests that this creates a paradoxical dilemma, for work becomes the source that nourishes and provides for the couple's existence, yet at the same time deprives the family of the time together required to maintain intimacy.[9] Because most mothers are now working on a part-time or full-time basis, there is less time for the couple and more need for the responsibilities of the home and the children to be shared. Mothers who work are caught in the dilemma of enjoying their work and the extra money available to the family, but feel guilty that they have less time to spend with their children. And when the conflict is defined as time demands from work versus time for the children, where does the marriage come in?

The label "workaholic" suggests that a person is involved with work not only to earn money but for the psychological benefits that come with feeling competent and productive. Several psychologists have suggested that many men feel uncomfortable with the level of closeness that their partners want, and/or the tasks required in parenting. Rather than trying to acknowledge and work with this situation, many men simply "let" their work demands take them away from the stressful feelings that family intimacy unleashes. This is especially likely to happen when work makes the man feel valued and important at the same time that his wife is making him feel inadequate.[10]

The pressures created by work may be just as much a reality of the workplace as they are an escape from intimacy. However, few people even question the power that organizations have over their lives and instead take out their frustration on each other. Like the other two-career couples studied by Barnes, I find myself adjusting my schedule to meet the work demands put on my husband. While there are some days when I can appreciate that this long workweek is not exactly my husband's idea of fun either, there are other times when I get caught up in exhaustion and frustration. It is not easy to accommodate his career in ways that compromise my own or to believe that my husband's loyalty is to his job rather than his family. Even when I don't want to blame my husband, it is hard not to. And aside from the sadness I feel on the days that our kids won't get to see their dad, I am also aware that I, too, am alone.

In my own marriage, as in the marriages of the two-career couples I have seen in marital therapy, a husband's overinvolvement in work leads to distance and conflict. When the couple is not able to face this situation together and turn to each other for support, the resentment becomes more deeply entrenched. Too often, a vicious cycle gets started, with the wife complaining and the husband spending even more time away. As you will see in Chapter Seven, marital conflict is always hard on the children. But there are other ways in which children in workaholic families can be affected. In some families, the moms get overly involved in their roles as mother, making up for the loneliness and disappointment they have in their roles as wives.[11] The children can also get caught up in excessive loyalty to their mothers, acting out and testing the relationship they have with their fathers. This was the case for the Sampson family.

THE SAMPSON FAMILY

It would have been impossible to predict at their wedding that such confident and hopeful individuals would be so unhappy five years later. Janet and Russel Sampson met as law students at one of the best universities in the country. Brilliant, well-liked by classmates, and socially popular, their future seemed secure in every way. Before they married, Janet and Russel talked about how they would balance careers and children. Even though they agreed that Janet would stay home until the youngest child started school, they both wanted to be involved parents. Russel declared that his family would come before his job, and that he would be home as much as possible to participate in raising his kids.

As luck would have it, Russel was transferred to the firm's main office the same month Janet discovered she was pregnant. They agreed to the move, as they knew it would ensure Russel's success at his new law firm. But the couple was far away from family and friends, and when the baby came, Janet found herself all alone. Despite Russel's promise to help, his cases developed one crisis after another that kept him at the office all day and most of the night. Janet grew increasingly exhausted, angry, and, finally, depressed. The worst moment came when Janet once again pleaded for Russel to come home early, only to be told that there was something wrong with her in not being able to manage a healthy baby like a normal woman.

Without realizing it, Russel had struck the most painful chord possible. Janet's mother had been preoccupied with her own interests and Janet's younger brother's sports commitments, and had had no time for Janet. When Janet needed a ride somewhere or a friendly ear to share a problem with, her mother had brushed her aside. Occasional illnesses were "not allowed." Janet recalled being left at home one night after throwing up because her mother needed to cheer for her brother at a basketball game. As Janet told me, "It wasn't even a championship or a playoff, just a regular game!" Janet learned to be self-sufficient and to rely on no one— that is, until she fell in love with Russel. By making it sound as if Janet was inadequate for needing him, Russel revived Janet's feelings of not being good enough to be loved. It seemed to Janet that Russel had chosen his work over her and their baby, much as her mother had preferred her son and had abandoned her daughter.

By the time they came for marriage therapy, the couple was in serious trouble. As predicted, Russel had received the job promotion and security he was aiming for, and was well respected in his firm. But Janet was bitter about his success. She claimed that Russel was addicted to his senior partners' praise, and would do anything for them. In contrast, she felt that she had to beg to get Russel to even consider the most basic request, and she resented his apparent disinterest in her and, by that time, their two children. Janet had long before stopped relying on Russel to be there for her emotionally, but felt that the children, now ages four and two and a half, desperately needed a father. Some weeks, the little ones would start their day hearing that Daddy had already left for the office and would fall asleep still asking, "When is Daddy coming home?"

Because Russel was rarely home, he did not understand the children as well as Janet did. Paula, the elder, was easily overstimulated, and would become wild and aggressive after Russel played tackle with her. Ryan was at an age where he was constantly testing the limits, and if Russel told him to hold his glass with two hands, Ryan would stare his father in the eye and dump the milk on the carpet. Of course it would be Janet's job to jump in and calm the children down. When Russel got angry and criticized the way Janet was raising the kids, Janet would counterattack by saying that the children didn't behave that way with her, and perhaps if Russel took the time to get to know them, they wouldn't behave that way with him either.

Although both Janet and Russel wanted to try to save the family, there was little affection or caring left between them. Russel was resentful that Janet could not celebrate his career success or recognize how hard he was working for the family. Janet scoffed that he didn't know how to set limits at work, and if asked, her choice was for him to get a less demanding job and spend more time at home. Each felt alone, unsupported, and unhappy even though, on the surface, all their dreams had come true.

When Children Come First: Child-Centered Families

Janet and Russel's challenge was similar to that faced by all young parents. In addition to protecting the relationship from work, each couple must learn how to preserve intimacy after the arrival of children. In the past few years, a number of psychologists have studied the specific changes that happen to the marriage through the pregnancy and subsequent adjustment to baby, toddler, and teen.[12] For some parents, changes are created by a diagnosis of infertility, as the challenge of conception abruptly alters the couple's way of relating as lovers. Making love is dictated by the rise and fall of the thermometer or the changes on a litmus strip. However, even couples who are spared the stress of creating a pregnancy find their lives dramatically altered once their baby arrives. Parents have less time to enjoy being alone with each other and have to redefine almost every aspect of their relationship.

It is not surprising that the first two years of parenting are the most stressful, and that many couples who dreamed of the joy of sharing a child start contemplating divorce. Psychologist Ron Taffel suggests that much of the strain and tension is created by the unequal ways in which men and women approach the responsibilities of parenting and managing the home. Despite years of exposure to equal rights, it is still the mother who takes on the bulk of the physical and psychological responsibilities of caretaking.[13] The father's life at home changes less dramatically, but he begins to experience a burden of greater financial responsibility, a situation that is made more urgent if the wife is taking an extended maternity leave or leaving work permanently. A pattern emerges in which the father spends more time at work and the mother feels abandoned at her time of greatest need. Wives become annoyed when they feel that they can't count on their husbands to help out more at home, and the couple's stress level soars. As a result, both spouses experience a decline in marital satisfaction and increased marital conflict. The crisis of the first newborn is a serious one, as 15 percent of couples are no longer living together within two years of their baby's birth.[14]

The marital stress that comes with a baby is often related to the sharp contrast between the partners' expectations of shared parenting and the realities of dividing unanticipated responsibilities. Yesterday's pattern of the husband earning money while the wife took care of the children is not a reality for most couples today, as the majority of mothers with young children work. Nor do most couples start their lives together agreeing to the stereo-types of Mom/Dad that prevailed thirty years ago. In most "post-modern" marriages, both partners pledge equality from the begin-ning of their relationship.[15] But the birth of a baby changes everything, and even the most liberated couples seem to slip back into the old, stereotyped roles. Both husband and wife resort to the patterns that were established in their own families of child-hood, even though at the same time they may feel deeply resentful. This is especially true for those woman who identified with their fathers' power and became very successful at work. Having a baby puts a woman in a different position, as she now experiences herself as a mother. Once again, the blueprint of her parents' marriage is revived, and she unknowingly accepts the kind of relationship she may have just a few years earlier protested most vigorously.

Different Kinds of Love

Few people realize how dramatically having a baby in the home decreases the time and energy spouses have for each other. While most people expect to be drawn more closely together by the birth of a baby, just the opposite can happen. Even though I remember the disappointment and arguments in my own marriage after our son was born, I was surprised to learn that many men begin extra-marital affairs around the time of the birth of a child.[16] In order to fully understand this, it is necessary to realize the power of intimacy to make a person feel wanted and special. Partners count on each other to feel valued and important. When this basic need is not met, it is easy for a partner to turn to an alternate source. While some men manage to get their need for affirmation met at work, others are susceptible to a romantic involvement to help them feel good about themselves.

There is another aspect to the challenge of adjusting to parenthood that I have found in my own life as well as in the lives of my clients. Most new mothers have a difficult time balancing the roles of wife and mother, especially when the baby is very young. Sleep deprivation usually adds to the mother's experience of being exhausted and overwhelmed. Because the baby's demands are real and urgent, it is normal for her to put her own needs second. But learning how to prioritize and balance her husband's need for her is complicated and stressful. Although most new fathers are thrilled with the addition to the family, they are not prepared to lose their intimacy with their partner.

If the couple is not able to find time to be alone together, the relationship suffers in important ways. Increasingly, the mother looks to feel validated from her new and important role of being a mother. At the same time, the father spends more time at work, or with new interests that help him maintain a sense of being special and important. Because the partners are not taking care of each other emotionally, they must learn to take care of themselves—a process that is usually accompanied by resentment and disappointment. Instead of joining together to meet the challenges of early parenting, spouses learn that they must fight for personal time. An air of competition is born, with each parent fighting to ensure that his or her private needs will be met. When parents turn into adversaries instead of friends, the children are in trouble.

THE SAMPSONS, CONTINUED

Janet and Russel, who were both successful lawyers before the children were born, were the best adversaries I have ever met. At home, and in our marital sessions, they would argue about the time they needed to exercise or to return phone calls. I often got so caught up in their eloquent and well-stated cases that I forgot I was supposed to be helping them talk *with* each other! Although they each thought that by making their point they would win, their adversarial position was killing their intimacy. When I asked Janet and Russel to describe a scene in the future where their dreams of the best life possible had come true, each talked to me about having fun together as a family. Even though the scenarios had different settings, the feeling of sharing and togetherness was vivid in both responses. I asked them to consider how their competitive mode would help them make this dream come true. Only then could they see how being adversaries would never help them build the family that they both wanted.

Sadly, marital tension and conflict is not a secret kept from the children. As I listened to Janet and Russel describe their children's acting-out behavior, I kept thinking about a research study by Phillip and Carolyn Cowan.[17] As part of their study, the Cowans kept in touch with the same families for ten years. In addition to meeting with the parents, they also assessed the children at different points in time, and even included teacher evaluations as part of their data. They found that when parents lose their marital closeness and become competitive, there is less warmth and responsiveness in the family. As toddlers, the children from these families were described as being more difficult. When they were evaluated a few years later, their kindergarten teachers reported that these children were having a harder time adjusting than their classmates. Happily, as Russel and Janet began to work together and try to appreciate each other's positions, they found ways to be more responsive and supportive. Within months, the children's behavior had settled down.

The Revival of Unhappy Memories

In their conversations with parents, the Cowans learned about another important issue that affected many families. Several of the couples who had seemed to be doing well before the pregnancy became stressed and unhappy during the transition from the end of the pregnancy through the first year of the child's life. These parents all reported that for one of them, the reality of having a baby had caused them to remember aspects of their childhood that they had not thought about for years. In all of these situations, there had been conflict, violence, or unhappiness in their families of origin. Becoming a parent had reawakened painful memories, causing the parent to become depressed and emotionally reactive. If the couple was not able to understand and work out the problems created by the past, they developed a stressful and conflicted relationship. Their children suffered withdrawn or aggressive behavior as toddlers and later had school problems as well.

Parenting as an Escape

For some couples, the close relationships they develop with their children help them escape from problems they are having in the marriage. While they might have wanted children in the expectation that parenting would bring them closer together, often this desire masked problems that were festering in the marriage. When the children do come, the unhappy parent often chooses to enjoy the relationship with the child rather than spend time in a marriage that feels stressful and unpleasant. For some, being with the children becomes an excuse used to avoid difficult aspects of the marriage. Rather than face a problem head-on, a parent might claim that his or her inability to be there for the partner was created by the excessive needs of the child. The partner is then left feeling selfish for wanting something from the marriage at the expense of his or her child. An extreme example of this can be found in the case of Lynn and Mark.

Lynn and Mark

Lynn and Mark had been married for ten years when they started marriage therapy with me. The couple had two daughters whom they described as being bright but shy and fearful. The younger child, Amy, was prone to nightmares and Lynn often wanted to console her and ended up spending the night sleeping in her daughter's bed.

Lynn had met Mark when she was a high school senior. Although he was ten years older than she, her parents had been approving of the relationship, and the couple had married in Lynn's sophomore year of college. Lynn's family had been overbearing and strict. Her Catholic school had reinforced her parents' values, so that Lynn described herself as having been completely naive and easily influenced when she met Mark. Mark, in contrast, was the eldest son of immigrant parents who had largely neglected him due to their all-consuming work obligations. Mark had dropped out of school in order to work and had been hugely successful. By the time he met Lynn, he was financially secure and well-established in his own business. Although he was not religious, he donated large amounts of money to his church—the same church that Lynn and her family attended.

Mark presented the image of a respectable, conservative man, but his private life was quite the opposite. Mark was very focused on sexual pleasure and had introduced Lynn to a wide range of sexual stimulants and practices. At the beginning of their relationship, Lynn had "gone along" with Mark, and had posed for private pictures, shared pornographic experiences, and had even taken drugs to heighten sexual pleasure. If Lynn was uncomfortable, she had cut off her awareness of these feelings. In the same way that she had followed her parents' demands to be a good girl in the ways they defined it, she let herself become the wife her husband desired.

Things started to change for Lynn after she became a mother. Because the girls were born two years apart, Mark had initially accepted Lynn's restrictions on their sexual relationship due to being pregnant, nursing, or totally exhausted. However, as the girls entered their preschool years, Mark became increasingly intolerant of Lynn's excuses that she was too tired for sex. Mark became fixed in his position that there would be no more children despite Lynn's wish to try for a son.

Lynn had told no one the details of their private life and how unhappy she was in her marriage. She had a beautiful home, two beautiful daughters, and a respected, successful husband. She also knew that her parents would never support or accept marital separation or divorce. Lynn was also not good at expressing her feelings and did not know how to negotiate for a different sex life. Mark was a gifted salesman and could use persuasion and charm to disarm all of Lynn's arguments. The only way out for Lynn was through her relationships with her daughters. When Amy started to have nightmares, Lynn responded by staying close to her daughter all night. Perhaps sensing her mother's anxiety and relief at their shared sleeping arrangement, Amy's nightmares persisted, leaving Mark alone in bed. He was unhappy with this situation, but caught in a bind. Lynn was the mother he had always wished for, providing their children with attention and care. So long as Amy really needed her mother, Lynn was off the hook.

Problems for Children

When children grow up in a home where their parents are not emotionally available to each other, they get the message that the most special things in life do not come from the marriage. Children, work, friends, or sports are recognized as areas of passion and commitment. The marriage, in contrast, seems empty and boring. When the lonely parent compensates for his or her partner's focus outside of their marriage by getting overly involved with the children, there are immediate harmful consequences. Young children may develop emotional or behavioral problems that "require" their parent to stay overly active. Older children have difficulty in maintaining friendships and suffer in other ways as well. Research has shown that teenagers who had a close relationship with one parent, and whose parents were not close with each other, have high degrees of depression and anxiety.[18] Friendships with peers can help mitigate some symptoms of depression, but even then, teens who fit this family profile were found to have anxiety and other emotional problems. The same thing was true for teenagers who reported that their parents were not close, but that one parent had a particularly close relationship with a grandparent. The research studies support what therapists have known for a long time: Children and teens who are overly involved with a parent have a harder time growing up. Problems persist into adulthood, and the grown children often repeat their parents' reliance on self-interests, extended family, or work to bring them happiness.

Parents who want the most for their children should look at the freedom their children truly have to focus on themselves, as children should. It is much easier to create an environment where this can happen when parents are fulfilled in their marriage. Establishing the priority of the marriage does not mean that all other commitments and loyalties are tossed aside, but it does mean that the partner's needs are constantly kept in sight. Even when there are competing demands, the partner and the marriage are respected.

If parents want their children to find happiness in life from a wife or a husband, they must look at the message they are sending by the example of their own marriage. When children see how much their parents value each other and their relationship, they are learning about an important source of fulfillment and gratification. A marriage that can be protected from the demands of other obligations is not taking away from the children, it is giving to them the expectation and hope that one day they, too, will have a loving partner.

QUESTIONS

1. How much time do the two of you spend by yourselves alone as a couple each week? Is it what you both want, or would one of you want to spend more or less time together?

2. Can you think of three things your partner does for you that make you feel special? Can you think of three things you do for your partner that he or she really appreciates?

3. When you think about your relationship before children and after children, what do you miss the most? What things have been added to your shared life?

4. How did your father show your mother how important she was to him? How did your mother show her love to your father? What would you say came first in their lives—work, children, obligations to their own family members, or the community? To what extent are these priorities echoed in your own life?

3

Teaching the Value
of Interdependence

*"Mom and I Are Always
There for Each Other"*

ONE OF THE MOST IMPORTANT lessons we want to teach our children is that they don't have to go through life alone. Ideally, the person they marry will be the one they can turn to for support. Just as a small child needs a parent to provide comfort and reassurance, so does an adult need a special person in her life to offer caring and encouragement. The importance of support in maintaining physical and mental health has been noted by researchers and therapists alike.[1]

It sounds like something every adult would want, but for most of the couples I have treated, mutual dependence has been extremely difficult to achieve. In our society, many adults struggle with the idea of becoming emotionally, physically, or financially dependent upon another. Today, more than ever before, independence has been stressed as an ideal to which all adults should aspire. Self-sufficiency is so heavily emphasized that many people expect to be able to achieve all their aspirations by themselves. Of course, in the arena of intimacy, this is counterproductive.[2]

I have been impressed by a number of recently published books and articles that focus on the meaning and consequences of independence for men.[3] For most of my years in practice, I have worked hard to help my male clients feel comfortable with a process that requires them to be self-aware and able to express their feelings. Most men are socialized to be in control and strong regardless of the situation and learn to shut themselves off from their feelings of vulnerability in order to comply. But when it comes to intimate relationships, vulnerable feelings are the norm. It has been sad and frustrating to see the extent to which men detach themselves from their emotions. Their efforts to fulfill the societal portrait of the ideal man collide with what is needed to establish mutual support.

While gender roles and gender socialization are important to most of the themes discussed in this book, they are critical to understanding the notions of support and dependency. Each of us could write a list of what the ideal woman would be like and a different one for the perfect man. If we compared our ideas, we might find a few differences—especially if we come from different generations, social classes, or ethnic backgrounds—but our lists would be more similar than different. For example, most people would describe the ideal woman as being nurturing, affectionate, and responsive to the emotional needs of others. Men, in contrast, would be defined as independent, competitive, assertive, and logical.[4] These differences do not have a biological or physiological basis, but are "learned" behaviors. When a man or a woman is molded to fit a role that does not necessarily complement their basic nature, the result too often is unhappiness or even psychiatric problems such as anxiety or depression.

Gender-determined roles influence how men and women approach dependency, and, in different ways, both are handicapped by the process.[5] If a man feels too feminine or vulnerable when he needs to be soothed or reassured, he will cut himself off from his feelings. Unfortunately, feelings don't just go away: they find expression in other outlets. It is not surprising that men who do not know how to tolerate difficult feelings turn to alcohol and other substances that can numb or distract. Pressure and stress that cannot be shared can also lead to health problems.[6] When men who are uncomfortable expressing their weakness are with women who display their vulnerabilities, they tend to want to escape or shut off the experience before their own repressed feelings are awakened. One response is to get angry. An alternative solution is to emotionally withdraw or shut down. Some men are so disconnected from their own tender emotions that they don't even have the vocabulary to describe their feelings. Talking becomes stressful rather than a relief because it is so hard for them to find the words to capture and release their inner experience. A conversation about feelings with a verbal, insightful wife simply adds to this sort of a man's sense of inadequacy and weakness.

The gender ideals reinforced in our society can work against women as well. As a result of their need for closeness, many women are reluctant to jeopardize close relationships through conflict, and may avoid even thinking about problems that could generate feelings of anger. Several psychologists suggest that women thrive through connection and become anxious at the thought of being rejected or left alone. As a result, they may have difficulty in asserting ideas and wishes that could jeopardize closeness. In the long run, this leads to a lack of authenticity, which makes genuine sharing and dependency impossible. It has also been suggested that women place the needs of other people first and feel selfish when they ask their partner to focus on them. And, of course, a woman who believes that she is unworthy does not feel entitled to ask that her own needs be recognized or met.[7]

Despite the fact that all men and women want to feel cared for, we have been socialized to accept or disavow certain aspects of dependency based on our sex. The differences start early in life, and include the way in which men and women are socialized to give and receive support. The whole idea of a supportive relationship is different for boys than it is for girls. Boys learn about support through sports and teams where they develop "side-by-side" relationships. Girls spend more time in activities that involve face-to-face interaction and sharing.[8] The differences are well ingrained by adulthood, for while women seek emotional and verbal connection, men are more comfortable doing things to demonstrate their caring. For example, men are more comfortable doing than talking, and express their affection in active ways, such as having sex or giving presents. Women describe intimate experiences as those in which personal thoughts and feelings have been shared. In conversations about problems, men try to come up with solutions rather than allowing a prolonged discussion of feelings.

However, both men and women long to be cared about, and feel angry and disappointed when their partner fails them. Things would be much easier if dependency didn't have so many negative associations. In an ideal world, the notion of turning to another for help when it is appropriate would be regarded as normal and growth-promoting rather than as an admission of weakness.[9] If partners could believe that the ability to rely on and be relied on would add to their marriage, they would have less resistance to expressing their needs.

The importance of becoming dependent on a partner in order to give and receive support is one of the factors that distinguishes happy marriages from those that dissolve or are experienced as dissatisfying. In order to make a marriage succeed, it is vital that the couple learn how to establish a sense of interconnection and mutual dependence, where each partner can genuinely rely on the other. Partners need to open up to each other in order to feel loved and supported. The most recent studies on intimacy show that one of the most important ingredients is mutual understanding. Partners who know how their spouse feels about a number of issues and who also believe that their spouse understands them are the couples who are most satisfied with their marriages.[10]

Psychologists Richard Mackey and Bernard O'Brien, who studied happy marriages that have passed the test of time, discovered that support does not happen automatically. In order to feel supported, spouses had to first learn to talk to their partners about the things that were on their minds. While most of the husbands started out being more comfortable doing rather than talking, over the years this changed dramatically. After twenty years of marriage, partners who were satisfied had learned how to talk together about a wide range of issues. The importance of learning how to talk about feelings has been confirmed in other research studies as well. Men who can acknowledge and tolerate uncomfortable feelings, such as sadness, are ultimately more affectionate in their marriages. Their ability to share feelings leads to marriages that are more stable and more satisfying to themselves and their wives.[11]

Children who grow up in a family where both parents can openly share feelings have a wonderful advantage. Fathers who are emotionally connected to their wives are also more likely to be emotionally connected to their children. This is particularly important because many men regret the lack of closeness they had with their own fathers. The father who is able to emotionally relate to his children has the opportunity to reverse the painful consequences of the suppression and denial of feelings he grew up with. The result is the freedom for children to turn to their fathers as well as their mothers for support and emotional guidance. A boy, especially, realizes that his father's openness does not diminish his power, but adds to the way in which he is respected. Learning to open up and express feelings becomes an option for the son as well.[12] This was an interesting by-product in the family I treated not too long ago.

Paul and Elaine

Like many men, Paul grew up in a family where men were considered strong, responsible, and rational. Perhaps this was more exaggerated in Paul's family, for his mother was an anxious woman who was prone to hysterical reactions. Insects would throw her into a state of panic, and if one of the children scraped a knee, she would scream so loud the neighbors would come running. Paul, like his father, laughed at these outbursts and became even more stoic and dismissive of his own feelings. By the time he met Elaine, in high school, Paul was already a focused, competent person who had assumed the caretaking role in his family. He continued this pattern in his relationship with Elaine, whose shy, self-doubting style struck a chord in his protective nature.

Although Elaine was more comfortable in exploring her feelings, this kind of discussion rarely occurred between them. Paul would accuse Elaine of rambling and getting off the subject, and he would become irritated and annoyed. As a result, Elaine kept many of her feelings to herself, but grew increasingly more distant. The more competent and focused Paul became, the more inadequate and depressed Elaine grew.

By the time this couple started marital therapy, there was a great deal of unacknowledged anger and resentment between them. Paul was intolerant of Elaine's shortcomings in managing money and the home, and Elaine silently resented Paul's domination and dismissive attitude toward her. Their children, great sources of happiness and pride, kept this couple together. However, the eldest, Benjamin, was entering adolescence and becoming increasingly withdrawn. He rarely talked about school or friends, and was sarcastic when his parents tried to learn more about his life.

After I learned about the couple's problems, which included infrequent sex and a lack of closeness, I asked them to assess how supportive they were of each other. Paul quickly answered that he was totally supportive of Elaine, and took care of almost all areas of her life. He was shocked when Elaine answered, "I don't feel at all supported by Paul. He may pay the bills and talk to repairmen, but I don't think he cares one bit about how I feel." When I asked Elaine whether she thought she was supportive of Paul she answered, "I would be if I thought he would take it from me." Paul amazed me by catching his breath before saying in a heartfelt voice, "That's what I want more than anything in the world."

Paul started to talk about how lonely he felt. The other men in the office where he worked would talk to their wives on the telephone, and he would hear them laughing or sharing what appeared to be an intimate moment. In contrast, Elaine never called him, and when they did talk, it was about chores that needed to be coordinated or other home-related tasks. Paul started to become angry, accusing Elaine of not being grateful for all that he had given her and for not giving back what he really needed.

Like many people, Paul found it easier to express anger than the underlying feelings of loneliness, but with some urging and support, he began to speak again of feeling unloved. His words seemed to resonate with Elaine's feelings as well, and she joined him in wishing they could find a way to relate differently. I commented to Paul that all his organizing and planning for the family seemed to be acts of love, and wondered how it was possible for a man who had so much love to give could have a wife who felt so unloved. At first it was difficult for Paul to understand, but as the couple continued to talk, Paul could see that Elaine felt diminished rather than supported when he took over. He could show more support for Elaine by listening to her point of view and to her feelings, even if she started to ramble and didn't get to the point in an efficient way. As Elaine explained, "I don't always know how I feel when I start talking, but if you give me a chance, you could help me so much just by listening."

Paul admitted that he had an even harder time knowing how he felt about anything. "I don't think I've ever taken the time to really think about my feelings. And I guess I've grown up believing that even if I had feelings, no one would do anything about them anyway." This had been the formula in Paul's parents' marriage, where feelings were either ridiculed or dismissed. As Paul told me more about his parents' marriage, I also saw the challenge he faced in admitting his dependency on Elaine. In Paul's family, women were viewed as being irrational and completely undependable, thus reinforcing the belief that men had to be totally self-sufficient. But this way of relating was not working for either Paul or Elaine, and as they realized the extent to which the past dictated their present, they became committed to creating a different marriage.

Our work in therapy helped Paul to realize the extent of his own vulnerable areas and anxieties, which he had previously avoided by overly focusing on Elaine's. It was not always easy for Elaine to listen and respond, as her perception of herself as helpless made her need a partner who was strong and caretaking. However, as Elaine began to experience her own strength and capabilities, she became more comfortable in allowing Paul to express his doubts, worries, and fears. Paul began to pride himself on his ability to stay with Elaine's discussions, and to offer support in the form of listening and caring rather than solving her problems or taking over.

During the time that the couple was becoming more expressive and supportive, an interesting change took place in Benjamin. After months of overhearing his parents talk and explore their reactions to different things, Benjamin suddenly started to communicate his own feelings. Benjamin was angry at both of his parents and had a scorecard of events they had unknowingly "mishandled." I'm not sure I could have done as good a job just listening to this list of accusations, and I was impressed with how patiently Elaine and Paul sat with their son. When Benjamin had finished, Paul simply said, "I'm so glad you've been able to tell us how you feel. It will make it possible to do things differently from now on." Benjamin's voice was heard on a more regular basis, and his sarcasm faded into the memory of a passing phase.

Being Emotionally Available to Our Children

If husbands are not able to tolerate their own feelings or the feelings of their wives, they surely will not know how to respond to their children's emotional vulnerability. Parents who want to help their children understand and conquer difficult emotions first need to be able to work with their own. Recent research has emphasized how important it is for parents to acknowledge and respond to their children's feelings. Partners who are emotionally intimate are sensitive to low-intensity emotions in their children and are able to help their kids talk about what is going on. If their children are sad or upset, they are able to empathize with the emotional upset and then help their kids think of ways to handle the situation.

In contrast, there are many families who are uncomfortable with emotions and tend to dismiss their children's reactions. These parents often love their children very much and want to be helpful, but because they do not know how to soothe their own feelings, they tend to deny or dismiss emotional upset in their kids. For example, they may try to distract their child by trying to make her laugh or by introducing a pleasant topic. They might convey a belief that bad feelings are not something to dwell on. Because feelings create discomfort for them, they easily get impatient and tell their child through words or gestures to "get over it." The child misses an opportunity to learn how to soothe unpleasant feelings and how to use the emotional realm as an important source of information.

But the consequences do not end there. When children are emotionally "coached" by their parents, they learn how to regulate their emotions and benefit in a number of ways. Because these children are not overwhelmed by feelings, they do not become emotionally disorganized when they are upset, and can focus their attention on necessary tasks such as schoolwork. In addition to getting along better with friends and schoolmates, they are less likely to develop behavior or health problems. They do better in school, too. In one study, children whose parents were emotionally responsive to them had higher reading and mathematics scores than children whose parents were emotionally dismissive.[13]

When the Child Becomes the Emotional Anchor

When women are not feeling emotionally connected to their partner, there are problems that ripple throughout the family. Psychologists Susan Whitbourne and Joyce Ebmeyer studied couples who were married for over twenty years to learn how two individuals adjust to each other over time. They found that in the early years of marriage, women whose partners had difficulty with closeness would try to compensate by prodding their husbands to talk, or by becoming acutely sensitive to their partners' subtle cues in order to respond to them. Over the years, most of these women gave up, describing themselves as burned out, and began looking elsewhere for closeness. Other women whose husbands had a low potential for intimacy initially denied their loneliness and tended to excuse their husband's preoccupation with other matters. But over time, the excuses wore thin, and eventually these women were able to recognize that they were never going to feel cared about and supported by their husbands in the ways they had hoped. Like the other women in the same situation, they ended up turning away from their partner, and searching for intimacy in other relationships.[14] While some parents turn to friends and siblings, there are others who, unfortunately, turn to their children. When a parent turns to a child for this kind of emotional sustenance, there are always problems.

It is natural for children to offer support and comfort to their parents, for it is in their best interest to have happy parents. While it is a strength to find this kind of capacity for empathy and compassion in a child, it is unfair and unhealthy for a child to be used to make up for the deficiencies of a marital relationship. The child ceases to be a child, and is given responsibilities he should be protected from for many years. Some children appear to do well in this situation, and become "little adults" who seem to be perfect. They may even enjoy being the "favorite child," with all the special attention that comes with the territory, but, in truth, they have been saddled with an unfair burden. Ultimately, being responsible for a parent's happiness demands that they sacrifice their own needs. Such was the case in the McNeil family.

THE MCNEIL FAMILY

The problem that brought Robert McNeil to my attention was his father's drinking. Edward McNeil had voluntarily gone to an outpatient program after his boss confronted him with his recent absences from work and his awareness of Ed's tendency to drink too much on the weekend. Edward, a quiet man, was a perfect employee in every other way and had immediately agreed. When the alcohol counselor suggested that Robert be involved in therapy, both of his parents were shocked. At age eleven, Robert was a "perfect" child: obedient, respectful, and a wonderful student. Robert's mother, Diane, could not imagine how she could have gotten through the ordeal of her husband's drinking without having such a sensitive, loving child.

Robert, himself, was mistrustful of meeting with me. The drawings he did for me were very controlled and technical. Unlike other children I have assessed, he had no comments to add to my observations. After he finished, I asked him if he would like to keep his pictures or if I could have them. Robert answered by crumpling his pictures into a ball and commenting, "They're no good anyway." When I asked Robert to talk to me about how things were going at home, he shrugged his shoulders and looked away. His discomfort in talking on a one-to-one basis made the session uncomfortable for both of us, and I could not break through what felt like a barrier of mistrust. Children from alcoholic families are often afraid to reveal the family secret, but I was concerned that Robert's problem was excessive and that he had underlying problems with low self-esteem. My recommendation was family therapy.

Robert was more relaxed in his parents' presence, but still a quiet and overly restrained child. He was well aware of his father's drinking binges, as he would go to his mother's room to stay with her when she cried if Ed stayed out late. Diane had hoped that Ed would be able to control his drinking without professional assistance. She was embarrassed that her family was having a problem, as it was important to her to maintain a good image in the community. Before Robert had been born, Diane had taught at the local school, and she was respected as an excellent mother and a helpful volunteer with the PTA. The fact that Robert was quiet was not of great concern to either parent, as neither Diane nor Ed felt they were outgoing individuals. But both parents were upset at my suggestion that Robert didn't seem to like aspects of himself and my concern that underneath his "perfect" veneer was a boy who had a lot of unexpressed feelings.

Aside from the drinking, there were other apparent problems in the marriage. Diane had married late in life, and didn't have that much in common with Ed. In addition to differences in ethnic background, their childhood families had different financial means. Ed had no interest in Diane's passion for music and art, and thought it was silly for Robert to have violin lessons and play duets with his mom. Ed's idea of a good time was watching a football game with the "boys," with plenty of pretzels and beer, an activity that Diane dismissed as a disgusting waste of time. From my perspective, Robert was caught in the middle, and he dutifully practiced his violin every day before heading out to the playing field to throw a football. The differences between his parents were never discussed; each just looked the other way while hoping that one day things would change. And while neither parent enjoyed the other, they both adored their son. However, as Ed's drinking got progressively worse, Robert was the one who filled in by making sure he was home so that his mom would not feel lonely. Whatever anger or resentment he had was trapped deep inside, and he went through life performing the actions of a perfect son without any connection to his feelings. Fortunately, the McNeils were able to get involved in the therapy process and deal with the marital tensions that for so long had trapped their son.

When the Parentified Child Grows Up

Unfortunately, the problems created by providing support to a parent who does not have sufficient intimacy in his or her marital relationship are not confined to childhood. The self-sacrifice and responsibility involved when a child is relied on in this way leads to resentment that may not fully emerge until the grown child begins to date and take risks with closeness. If being intimate means losing yourself in order to take care of someone else, then intimacy is not worth seeking. Children who have taken on too much responsibility for supporting a parent often avoid adult commitment, or choose a partner whose neediness forces them to continue in a caretaking mode. Very often they are attracted to people who mistrust or resent intimacy, and, without intending to, repeat their parents' marriage.

A fear of getting too close to another person can also develop when a person's earlier life experiences have taught him to be mistrustful. Depending on another person for care and comfort creates a state of vulnerability, as there will inevitably be disappointment if the partner can't or won't cooperate. Because there is always a risk of rejection or disappointment, each spouse has to trust in the good intentions of the partner. If a person has been badly disappointed by others, he will be less likely to take that risk. It is much safer to deny the importance of the much wanted nourishment than to acknowledge desire and then experience deprivation.[15] Perhaps this is one reason why children who have lost a parent in childhood so often have difficulty in becoming dependent on another person. However, children who watch their parents withhold from each other also grow up questioning whether they can trust anyone to be responsive to their needs.

This is what happened to Irene and Bob.

IRENE AND BOB

Irene and Bob had been in marriage therapy once before, but had dropped out after five sessions. Now, six years later, they were totally miserable and on the verge of a divorce. Irene dreaded the thought of announcing a marital separation, as she was a very private person who resented other people knowing her business. Bob, although lonely and unhappy, still hoped that the marriage of thirty years could be saved. The couple agreed that their main problem was communication: They simply could not solve their differences. When the couple could not reach a decision that both could live with, Bob would ultimately get angry and Irene would retreat for weeks at a time. Over the years, these episodes of tension and distance had taken over the relationship, and the couple's closeness had dwindled to near extinction.

Irene and Bob had met at a mutual friend's house when they were in their early twenties. Although they were an attractive couple, it was a case of physical opposites attracting: Bob was dark and very tall, Irene petite and fair. Their family backgrounds were also very different, with Bob the eldest son in a working-class family and Irene the daughter of a financially successful businessman. However, they both were extremely bright and witty and, when on a few occasions the tension between them lightened, they both had smiles that were wonderfully infectious.

Bob's father had died suddenly when Bob was eleven years old, leaving his mother with no life insurance and three children to raise. Although she had remarried when Bob was sixteen, there had been several stressful years. Bob had taken on as many jobs as he could manage in order to supplement his mother's paycheck and thus feed the family. But, more important, Bob had become the "man" of the family. In this capacity, his mother would talk to him about her day-to-day struggles and worries.

Irene's family was financially affluent but emotionally turbulent. According to Irene, her father had an explosive temper and was prone to outbursts of screaming and shouting. The target of most of his anger was his wife, whom he viewed as being incompetent and needy. Her requests for help or attention would evoke sarcasm or rage, and he scorned her for the slightest weakness. Irene was his favorite child, chosen for her intelligence, her beauty, and her ability to stand up to him when challenged. Growing up with her parents' arguments was very stressful for Irene, partially because her mother made repeated attempts to get her daughter to protect her and side with her. In her mind, Irene rejected both of them, but particularly despised the desperate neediness that her mother represented.

Sometimes couples reveal more in their actions than in their words. In our second session, Bob's gold chain fell to his lap. He spent the next five minutes clumsily trying to attach the clasp around his neck while he participated in the conversation. Finally I interrupted him and asked if he had thought of turning to Irene for help. He looked shocked at my question and answered that the idea had never occurred to him. When I asked Irene if self-sufficiency went in both directions or was exclusive to Bob, she answered that she could hardly remember asking her husband for anything. She had always made sure that she could take care of herself. The few years that she had stopped working to look after their two children had been very difficult for her, and she had found a job that allowed her access to her own money as quickly as possible.

When I learned about Bob's excessive childhood responsibilities, I thought I had some understanding of his need for independence. Without intending to, his mother had stripped him of the freedom enjoyed by most adolescents, and he had felt smothered by her worries and needs. As a consequence of her husband's sudden and unexpected death, she had always kept tabs on Bob's whereabouts, demanding to know where he was going and exactly when he would return home. Needless to say, she was extremely anxious if he was even five minutes late. But Bob was a dutiful son, and although he resented his mother's anxiety and need for closeness, he had never rebelled. But this was only half of the picture. When I asked Bob about his parents' marriage before his father died, he said that he remembered almost nothing. He explained that he had so few memories of his father that anything he might say would be based on stories he had heard from others.

As I continued to probe for recollections, the veneer of Bob's calm exterior started to crack. Tears came to his eyes—even though when I pointed this out to him, Bob said he had no idea why he might be crying. I asked Bob if he thought he had ever grieved for his father and felt the pain of losing this special person at such a young age. Bob returned to his stony composure, and thought that he probably hadn't, given that his mother had been so overcome with grief and had needed him to keep the family running. I suggested to Bob that he probably had a great many complicated and painful feelings inside, feelings that belonged to an eleven-year-old child whose daddy had left him. His challenge in life was to learn how to accept these feelings in order to get rid of a burden that was exhausting him, and in order to believe that he could get close to Irene without the fear that she, too, would leave.

After listening to this, Irene commented that Bob's stony denial of feelings was probably the biggest problem in their marriage. It made him unavailable to her as a friend, as he was intolerant of her feelings as well as his own. All discussions were ended the minute they became emotionally pitched. I pointed out to Irene that Bob's self-sufficiency and rational perspective were not new qualities, but had been an obvious part of him when they dated and decided to marry. What did these qualities bring to her life that made Bob a safe person to love? Irene started to talk about her parents and how she had felt trapped by both of them. Her father had imposed his will on her choice of friends and hobbies, and was not a person who was easily challenged. Her mother always seemed to be trying to make friends with her, but Irene was suspicious of her real motives. Irene felt that if she let her, her mother would try to possess her and occupy all of her time. In these ways Irene also had felt suffocated by other people's needs and robbed of her right to lead her own life. Irene had also learned that it was not safe to reveal any flaws. Her memories of her parents' marriage made her fear that Bob might ridicule her or demean her if she exposed the slightest weakness. Above all, Irene had despised her mother's vulnerability and her father's anger.

Bob was a person whose calm demeanor made Irene feel secure. As long as things were going smoothly between them, Irene felt safe and content. But when she began to feel angry or hurt, she became highly agitated and unhappy with herself. With very little interpretation on my part, Irene could quickly see that she hated the angry part of herself that reminded her of her father, and the vulnerable side of herself that represented her mother. She could also see that Bob's self-sufficiency had led her to believe that, contrary to her childhood experiences, in this relationship no demands would be made on her. Bob's cool facade had initially appealed to her, as it kept the feeling side of her in check as well. However, when things were not going well, there was no way for either of them to process and discuss feelings that had to be recognized in order to achieve understanding and an acceptable solution.

Reciprocity

Developing mutual dependency or interdependence in a marriage also involves reciprocity. Partners develop an unspoken contract that balances the flow of give and take, leading to a sense of equity. This quid pro quo allows for fairness, as each partner takes turn in providing different services on behalf of the other and the relationship. In this way, each partner can make self-sacrifices on the other's behalf based on the expectation that at another time, or in another way, the partner will do likewise. When things work out well, partners feel that they are not alone in life or are totally responsible for their own well-being. Instead, there is a sense of mutual well-being and mutual caretaking. Studies on successful long-term marriages and marital satisfaction continuously point to equity and fairness as one of the most important factors.[16]

Over the years, I have learned that spending time with a couple who has developed this kind of mutual support is very enjoyable. The partners' commitment to each other's well-being is obvious and is confirmed by their emotional receptivity and responsiveness. The more that partners give to each other, the more there seems to be something to have and to give in turn. Children who grow up in this kind of environment watch how their parents are able to turn to each other in bad times. They can feel the closeness that has developed between their parents from this mutual caretaking. In the eyes of these children, marriage is a place where people are protected, loved, and supported.

The family environment that can be built from a supportive marriage is one in which children can also be more easily nourished and cared for. Because they are so sensitive to the general mood in the family, children flourish when their parents support each other. In fact, psychological studies with infants have shown that parents who are supportive of each other are more sensitive caregivers and raise children who seem more secure. Children from these families had fewer problems and showed a healthier adaptation to life.[17]

When parents support each other, the marriage becomes a resource that enables the partners to cope with stress and problems outside of the marriage. Many people in happy marriages have endured horrific problems, including poverty, racism, life-threatening illnesses, and physical handicaps. But rather than allow adversity to strain the marriage, couples who know how to depend on each other find that a loving, supportive relationship helps them cope with the most demanding challenges. I would like to tell you about a family I once knew whose ability to support each other in a time of crisis was truly remarkable.

STEVEN LEWIS

My favorite neurologist at the Hospital for Sick Children approached me cautiously one day. "I know you don't usually work with my patients who have muscular dystrophy, but could you do me a favor and stop by the clinic this afternoon? I have bad news for a family I've known a long time." Steven, age nine, was the third of four children in this family and the youngest son. His elder brother had been diagnosed with Duchenne's disease when he was just starting school, and had been in a wheelchair for five years. Genetic counseling had found a family connection from previous generations on both sides, although neither parent had grown up with an immediate family member who had this disease. The parents had learned that Duchenne's disease was more prevalent in boys than in girls, but that there were usually signs by the time a child was six or seven. The family had pulled together to help their elder son, David, learn to cope with his progressive loss of muscle strength. Silently, they cheered as Steven passed his seventh and eighth birthdays, climbing trees and hitting home runs. But lately Steven had started to trip and fall down, and the family was thrown back into the memories of David's early symptoms.

I sat in on the family's appointment with the doctor that day— the day that Steven's diagnosis was confirmed. Unlike other children who learn about their condition gradually, Steven knew exactly what his future would be like. He was the one who often helped his elder brother get dressed, and he was the one who wheeled him into the backyard. Now the family had to face the grim future of helping two sons become invalids, and live with the reality of an early death for both of their boys. As the doctor confirmed what everyone already knew, Steven's parents held hands and locked eyes through their tears. They had not lost their faith in God, but they did not look for miracles either. There was an acceptance of the life that God had given them, and a strength from standing together. Steve's mom, Alice, told me that she had plenty of down days, but somehow Frank was always there to give her a shoulder to cry on. And when Frank was not coping well, she always knew that as long as she was able to comfort him, they would get through it together.

They took some hope from the doctor's observation that because Steven had been older than most children when he first developed symptoms, his decline might also be more gradual, but they knew that their son's days of chasing baseballs were numbered. Frank said to me, "We work with what we have. As long as Steven loves baseball, there's no reason we can't watch the games together, and he can keep working on his card collection as long as he wants. Life is different from a wheelchair, but as long as you have a family that loves you, there's every reason to keep on going." Despite their pain and struggles, Frank and Alice still laughed together and took time to go out alone. Their determination to make the most of what they had kept their marriage and their family strong and vibrant.

Learning to Depend on Others

In marriages where partners do not offer mutual support, partners have become disappointed in each other and have come to believe that they must look out for themselves first. When I meet with this kind of couple, I hear spouses complain that their partner is selfish or self-centered. Spouses act on an individual basis and there are few instances of seeking or providing emotional tenderness. Support is only offered in areas that do not compete or detract from each individual's priorities.

Couples who have difficulty in this area also frequently talk to me about their belief that anything they ask their partner for will be held against them. In this kind of marriage, there is a similar sense of mistrust based on a fear of obligation. If a favor is given, then a favor is owed. Underlying this fear is the expectation of exploitation, and the dread that what might be asked for in exchange will exceed the benefit of what is received.

Children raised in this family environment are very aware of the separateness of their parents. Even if there is not overt conflict, they can see that their parents do not trust each other with their innermost selves. The belief that you can rely only on yourself permeates daily living, and teaches the child to similarly avoid dependency. A child who grows up with this lesson learns that marriage is a place where one must always keep one's guard up. After hearing repeatedly how selfish their mother or father is, they may come to believe that people are exploitive and that self-sufficiency is the safest road to follow.

If children are to grow up believing in a future where their needs will be respected and their love will be received and responded to, they must see this in their parents' marriage. When parents are able to offer each other support and caring, they create an environment where there are emotional resources that benefit all the family members. Most important, they teach their children that people can be trusted and relied on.

QUESTIONS

1. Who do you turn to when you are upset and want to talk? If you try to talk to your partner, do things seem better or worse?

2. Are you more comfortable with facts or feelings? Is your partner more comfortable with facts or feelings?

3. Does your partner really listen to you when you talk? Do you think your partner remembers the things that have troubled or upset you in the past?

4. In what ways does your partner make you feel better when you are upset? What do you do for your partner?

5. How often do your children know the details of things that have been upsetting to either you or your partner? How often did you know these details about your own parents?

4

Instilling the Importance
of Mutual Respect

*"Marrying Your Mom/Dad Was
the Best Thing I Ever Did"*

THERE ARE MANY THERAPISTS who believe that self-esteem
is the cornerstone of mental health. With healthy self-
esteem comes the courage to venture out, take risks, and participate fully in life. Due to its importance, clinicians and researchers
have concentrated on understanding how a child develops self-
esteem and how parents can encourage confidence in their children. Heinz Kohut, a psychoanalyst who developed a branch of
analysis known as "self-psychology," stressed the importance of a
consistent caretaker who could serve as a "mirror" to validate the
child's feelings of importance and worthiness.[1] While the relationship between child and parent undoubtedly contributes to a
child's sense of well-being, children are also deeply affected by
the ways in which parents demonstrate respect for each other.

Respect is learned through observation, but also, and more important, through identification. As children develop psychologically, they "take on" aspects of their parents through the process of identification. The child may begin by imitating a certain attribute, but he eventually comes to view it as being an integrated part of himself. A mother who is filled with self-doubt provides little self-confidence for her child to absorb or wish to identify with.

Children are very aware of the respect each parent has for himself and for the other. Through actions and words, spouses communicate how much they appreciate and value each other. The child, imagining herself playing her parent's role as mother or father, forms an identification and view of self that includes perceived esteem. When parents praise or compliment each other, they send a message of value that is fully absorbed by the child. When parents demean each other, they create discomfort and conflict in the child.

There are other ways that self-esteem is revealed in marital interactions. An adult who feels good about himself expects to be treated by others in a fair, respectful way and is able to assert himself to ensure this. Similarly, an adult who feels good about himself does not need to demean his partner in order to feel better. The result of such an interaction is that both parents become tarnished and problematic sources of identification.

Disrespect between parents also creates an imprint of marriage as an unsafe place to be. Most children grow up yearning to feel valued and successful, and while their talents and efforts may lead them to excel in many areas of life, be it sports, school, or music, the skills needed to establish an intimate relationship do not rest on these accomplishments. As we have seen, the adult who is learning to become part of a couple will unconsciously turn to the memories and blueprint of his parents' marriage. Experiences of seeing parents humiliated or disrespected by each other create an expectation and a fear that this is how married adults treat their partners. When parents erode each other's self-respect, the results can be devastating to the child.

Although the process of two adults devaluing each other creates a disturbing image, the outcome is equally if not more dangerous if only one parent is devalued. In this situation, the sex of the deval-ued parent and the sex of the child need to be considered. Although there are many possible outcomes, the clients I have worked with have demonstrated specific patterns that may be common to others.

Daughters and Disrespected Mothers

The link between mothers and daughters should be straight-forward because the mother is the child's first love object. Lov-ing mom and becoming just like mom can easily go hand in hand. But when a daughter observes that the woman she adores is not admired by others, her relationship and her identification become tested and strained. The situation is made even more injurious when the slings and arrows come from her father's bow.

If a wife is devalued by her husband, their daughter has two choices. The first is to choose to identify more closely with her mother and compromise her own potential. Her partner will be someone she can value more than herself, and she is more likely to repeat her mother's unhappiness. Her other choice is to choose to identify more closely with her father and follow his path to success. She may excel in school, business, and friend-ships, but when it comes to love, she will have predictable prob-lems. Any relationship that too closely resembles her parents' marriage will revive the blueprint of how her mother was treated by her father. Her fear of becoming her mother in a world where only husbands can excel and be happy will make intimacy almost impossible.

SUSAN

Susan started therapy with me after a miserable blind date with a man who had been described by friends as "Mr. Perfect." She could see why her friends had found him attractive and interesting, but for reasons she did not fully understand she found him dull and stressful to be with. Her discomfort had led to too much drinking and she had behaved badly. At age thirty-five, Susan was successful in her media career but lonely in her personal life. Her only meaningful relationship had been a brief long-distance affair that had started on a vacation in Italy. In general, she found herself attracted to European men but totally "turned off" by the American men she met.

Susan prided herself on being a creative and energetic person. An attractive although slightly overweight woman, Susan was strongly committed to her career and had achieved several promotions in a relatively short time. She had a few close girlfriends, but almost all were engaged or newly married. Susan felt left out but also bored by their "domestic" interests. Their plans to have children were equally disturbing to her; she could not imagine how becoming a wife and a mother was fun or enjoyable.

In therapy, Susan was initially reluctant to talk about her family life when she was a child. She described her father as a bright, lively businessman who was successful in all aspects of his life. His work often took him to Europe and he would come home with dolls and treats for his only child. In contrast, Susan's mother was described as being a boring, depressed woman who had essentially wasted her life. Susan paused when I asked her what she had learned about intimacy from her parents' marriage. She responded that her father did not act like he liked his wife very much and that he certainly had no respect for her. "No one thought that she made any worthwhile contribution or that there was anything special about her."

In my opinion, Susan's problems with dating were very much connected to her feelings about her mother. Susan's dislike of her mother was very apparent. In her apartment, she had a framed picture of her father with his arms around an attractive, laughing woman. Although most of her friends assumed this was a portrait of her parents, it was, in fact, a photo of her father with a neighbor. Susan said, "I always used to imagine that someone else was really my mother—someone more sophisticated and interesting."

Although some of Susan's feelings about her mother were a product of the mother-daughter relationship, it became apparent to me that Susan's father had treated his wife in a disrespectful and neglectful manner. Susan thought that her parents probably would have been divorced if they had not had a child. She remembered her father berating her mother and calling her stupid to her face and behind her back. He was the one with flair and ideas; she offered little, and went along with his plans. When her husband was traveling, she was especially subdued.

Susan and I began to explore what she had learned about being a wife from watching her parents' marriage. Susan's mother's decision to not work was typical for a woman of her generation and economic standing, but in Susan's family it had fueled a total lack of respect. Susan's father was viewed as interesting and accomplished, her mother as boring and useless. In Susan's eyes, and I suspected in her parents' eyes as well, the father possessed all the vigor and worthwhile characteristics. He looked down on his wife and encouraged his daughter to view her in a similar way. Her mother's inability to stand up for herself led Susan to believe that wives are not valuable people, but are inadequate women with empty lives.

Even though Susan did not admire her mother, she had already formed an identification with her. Whether she liked it or not, there were parts of her that made Susan her mother's daughter. As Susan got older, it became more important to disidentify with her mother by proving through her accomplishments that she was not at all like her. Her career and her vacations in Europe strengthened her identity with her father.

In therapy, I helped Susan connect her dislike of American men to the lesson she had learned from her parents' marriage. Susan's discomfort in dating American men showed how scared she was of being "forced" to lead the unhappy life of her mother. The boredom she felt on dates came from the part of her that had identified with her mother. With support, she was able to talk about her fears of losing her self-respect and vitality like her mother had. As she began to understand how her fears of intimacy were based on assumptions she had never challenged, she became less guarded and more receptive to the men in her immediate environment. Although the change process would take a long time, she no longer believed that to love a man would lead her to lose everything she cherished.

Sons and Disrespected Mothers

Male children are also affected by a marriage in which the wife is not treated respectfully. Although it is easier for them to identify with the successful father, they often struggle with feelings of guilt for allowing their mother to be treated badly. They may also question the appeal of marriage if all women are viewed as basically incompetent or unimportant. They may be attracted to a strong woman, but feel too threatened to allow intimacy to develop. The threat comes from the blueprint of the parents' marriage where only one partner was allowed to excel and be recognized. To love a woman who is not inferior means risking the unquestioned right and security of superiority. Too often, the son who carries a blueprint of a marriage with unbalanced respect chooses a partner who in many ways is inadequate and relies on his strength. His caretaking allows him to relieve the guilt he feels in relation to his mother, but, eventually, his burden leads to resentment and a disrespectful attitude toward the unequal partner he has chosen. That is exactly what happened to Roy and Jan.

ROY AND JAN

Roy met Jan while she was working as a waitress during a summer recess from college. Although Roy ate lunch in the same booth every day, Jan paid little attention to him. However, one day Roy brought his two young sons, and Jan saw a caring and gentle side to a man who was usually abrupt and aloof. After that day, Jan was more interested in her regular customer, and listened attentively as he told her about his ex-wife's drug problems and how he had taken on sole custody of the children. Roy asked Jan out after work one day, and two weeks later she moved into his home.

Jan was the eldest of three children whose parents drank and partied excessively and who were largely unavailable to her. Her mother was a strong, competitive woman who had criticized all aspects of her daughter's life. Until she met Roy, Jan felt that she was worthless. Roy's interest in her was like an antidote to her mother's poison, and she treasured him as the best thing that had ever happened to her. Although Roy was opinionated and sometimes stubborn, Jan deferred to him in order to keep the peace.

In the beginning of their marriage, Roy enjoyed taking care of Jan. Eventually he wished she could do more on her own, and tried to help her get organized. For example, Roy would give Jan a list of errands that needed to be attended to as a way of helping her focus on her household responsibilities. Jan secretly resented Roy's lists and his superior attitude, but was afraid of making him angry. Although she tried to keep her feelings inside, she began to feel less and less like having sex, and started to "forget" things on Roy's lists.

The couple started marriage therapy with me just after their third anniversary. Roy initiated the therapy to get help with their sex life, and to get help with Jan's "attitude" problem. Roy's complaints about Jan were communicated passionately in our first five minutes together. "Why can't she keep the checking account straight? Why do our plants always dry up and die? Why does she just expect that we can take a summer vacation when she has no idea about our financial picture?" It was clear that Roy resented Jan's shortcomings, and felt alone in providing for the family.

In trying to better understand their life together, I had to know more about the childhood experiences of both partners. Roy had been an only child of parents who were both artists. His father was quite successful, but was a moody man who was volatile and unpredictable. Roy told me that his mother should never have had children—she had no interest in them, and had no maternal instincts. His mother rarely shopped for food or cooked, and could not keep track of his school projects or assignments. Roy's father was often enraged that things could not be better organized, but was not willing to change his own lifestyle to accommodate his son's needs. As a result, Roy's parents often fought about caretaking responsibilities, leaving all family members feeling angry and resentful of each other. As he got older, Roy spent increasingly less time with his parents and was basically on his own by the time he was sixteen. Unfortunately, Roy's friends were all drug users, and due to active drug use Roy barely managed to get his high school diploma.

As we talked about Roy's early home life, it became clear to me that Roy had never had an experience in which a woman could be depended on. His parents' preoccupation with their own lives had left him unable to trust anyone or to believe that another person could truly care about him. Roy had met his first wife in an addiction rehabilitation program, and described her as a self-absorbed person who demonstrated little affection but had made few demands. When his wife relapsed after their second child was born, Roy saw no reason to keep the family together. The children had not seen their natural mother for five years and she had made no attempt to visit them.

Jan suffered from low self-esteem, but she was a warm woman with strong nurturing instincts. She immediately made room in her heart for two sons, but because she had no experience with small children found that keeping them on schedule and the house organized was extremely difficult. In addition, the children tested her authority and often went over her head to get their dad's input— especially when they hoped his decision would be different. Roy's commitment to the well-being of his children gave him the strength to stay sober and to become competent at work, and he enjoyed giving them the attention he had never received as a child. As I learned more about the details of their home life, I could see that on some level Roy was afraid of losing his children's dependency and adoration, and he often gave the boys mixed messages about respecting Jan or abiding by her decisions instead of calling him at work. On the one hand, he desperately wanted Jan to run the home more efficiently so he could focus on his work, but on the other hand, he could not give up the caretaking position, which was psychologically gratifying and strength-promoting. In a similar way, Roy seemed to enjoy taking over when Jan was overwhelmed, while all the time resenting his burden. As we spoke, Roy could see that his tirades to Jan about her incompetence were an almost identical replay of his father's explosions against his mother.

As a child, Jan had faced physical abuse whenever she had protested her parents' actions, and she was initially very reluctant to express her accumulated resentment at Roy's controlling style. However, once she was able to talk about her feelings, the tension and distance between them began to shrink. Roy became more aware of the ways in which he could support Jan without diminishing her confidence, and Jan grew more able to confront Roy whenever she felt that he was putting her down.

In therapy, we talked about ways for the couple to establish Jan's position as an authority to the boys and to generate their respect. I suggested that it was not only the boys who needed to test Jan's ability to "be there," but also Roy's. Roy realized that as long as he belittled Jan she would never be perceived as a source of strength to either him or his boys. His challenge was to trust that Jan was willing and able to take care of his emotional needs as well. Once Jan understood the importance of persevering, she was able to confront Roy when he pulled away or tried to start a fight instead of confiding in her when there were tensions at work.

A turning point occurred when Roy was at home and his elder son, Richard, disregarded Jan's attempt to get him to take a bath. Before therapy, Roy might have taken over for Jan, as Richard would typically respond to his father. This time, rather then intervene, Roy watched Jan call Richard back into the bathroom and enforce the rules she had set. Only after Richard was in the tub did Roy add his opinion, making it clear to Richard that Jan knew what she was doing and that he expected his son to treat her with more respect.

Working with Roy and Jan was gratifying on two accounts. I watched a couple learn to support each other and build affection into a marriage that was originally tense and strained. But I also got to hear wonderful reports about the changes in the children as they settled down and started to accept and enjoy the strengths of their new mother.

Sons and Disrespected Fathers

Although there are many instances of working men looking down on their homemaking spouses, a steady job does not always protect a husband from being degraded by his wife. There are many families in which the wife disrespects her husband. In some instances, the put-downs are subtle but persistent; in other cases, the wives are openly insulting and degrading. In both situations, the children are deeply affected.

When a father is devalued, the son is left with intense, conflicting feelings. As Freud suggested in his Oedipal complex theory, every boy falls in love with his mother and wishes he could claim all her affection. He competes with his father and hopes that either his father will die or that his mother will lose interest in her husband. In healthy families, the father does not go away or lose his wife's love, and eventually the boy accepts his father's strengths and his pivotal relationship with his mother. In fact, he grows by acknowledging his father's capabilities and by striving to become more like him. If the mother devalues the father, then the boy's fantasy that he has won her heart prevails, leaving the boy with intense feelings of guilt for having stolen something precious from his father. He also will not respect and will not try to become like his father, for in his eyes, his father is a failure. The son who is deeply loved by his mother in a family where the father is not respected may succeed in many areas of his life and may appear to be confident and self-assured. However, the prospect of becoming a husband, and eventually a father, stimulates guilt and anxiety that can profoundly upset a relationship.

TOM AND PATRICIA

A case in point is Tom, whose wife, Patricia, called me in a state of panic. They had been married two years, and in many ways thought they had a perfect marriage. The couple had met in college, where they both participated in sports. Their shared interests and mutual admiration had been a good formula, and they rarely fought. That is, until Patricia started to talk about getting pregnant and starting a family. Although they had talked before marriage about how wonderful it would be to have children, Tom said he was feeling differently about it now. Despite the fact that he did not understand his feelings, he said that he felt pressured and unhappy, and asked for a divorce. Tom thought the best plan was for Patricia to find a new husband who wanted children as badly as she did, and to end their relationship.

Tom reluctantly agreed to marital therapy, but was uncomfortable talking about his feelings. He decided he owed it to both of them to try to figure out his position, and reluctantly started to answer my questions about his childhood. Tom initially stated that his family was perfect. His father was a well-liked professional in their community, and his mother was a respected woman who was active in charity work. When I asked Tom to tell me about his parents' marriage, he thought they were relatively happy but that in some ways his mother deserved more. Tom explained that his mother's family had been financially successful, while his father was the son of immigrants who had struggled to help their children find a better life. Tom's mother criticized her husband's table manners, choice of clothing, and lack of interest in the theater. Although Tom's father was highly regarded in the community, he was not respected in his marriage. Tom quietly revealed that his father seemed uncomfortable in his wife's presence and took up gardening as a hobby to kept him out of her "kingdom." The children would go only to their mother for advice. "Mom had a way of communicating that Dad really didn't know what was going on or the best way to handle things. She really ran the house." As her favorite son, Tom remembered his mom going to all of his high school athletic events, and how hard he had worked to make her proud of him. "I guess I was much closer to my mother than my father, but she is a unique woman, and I still feel lucky to have her for my mom."

I asked Tom to consider if his reaction to Patricia's wish for children could be in some way related to his blueprint of a father's worth in a family. When Tom was asked to imagine family life with children ten years from now, Tom immediately said that Patricia would probably be highly competent and organized, much as his mother was. He then grew somber as he realized that he could not describe himself in that picture, and that his image of Patricia happily being a mother meant that he was alone and not part of the family. Tears came to his eyes as he described his fear that Patricia would become the competent parent, and that he would be pushed out and disrespected like his father had been. He was afraid that Patricia would love the children and lose interest in him. Without realizing it, he had assumed that his destiny was to repeat his parents' marriage.

Daughters and Disrespected Fathers

Girls are also deeply affected when a mother looks down on their father. The wife who doesn't respect her husband communicates to her daughters that marriage is a disappointment, and that a woman cannot be made happy by a man. Rather than show her daughter how parents can work together to solve problems and strengthen a relationship, she teaches her daughter how misery compounds itself. The daughter of such parents may look unrealistically for the "perfect man" in order to defy her mother's fate. This is doomed to fail, for when he ultimately does show some weakness, she will not know how to offer support, encouragement, or acceptance. Her beliefs established in childhood that men are basically incompetent will resurface and influence her outlook. In fact, she is likely to overreact to minor problems and struggle with two conflicting options. Either she puts on rose-colored glasses and disregards issues that probably need to be talked about, or she overreacts and views small issues as major catastrophes.

The alternative solution for a daughter whose father was devalued is to choose a partner who, from the outset, disappoints her. She may know from the beginning that there are things about her boyfriend that don't appeal to her, but she continues in the relationship despite her reservations. When these issues surface after the marriage, she has an excuse to remain distant and displeased, just like her mother. Rose and Marvin's marriage shows how this can happen.

ROSE AND MARVIN

Rose and Marvin were in their early sixties when they approached me for marital therapy. Rose was an only child from a family that had once been affluent. Rose's father had been regarded as a "playboy" who spent money impulsively and gambled. Rose was very aware of her mother's disappointment in her father. She often witnessed her mother scolding him and could imitate her mother's sarcastic, condescending voice. Rose remembered feeling torn between her father's reckless but fun-filled approach to life and her mother's always somber, negative outlook.

Marvin had appealed to her because of his happy-go-lucky style combined with his traditional family values and his respect for hard work. However, Marvin lost his job in management after the couple had been married a few years, and drifted from job to job, never seeming to fit in. Rose refused to cut back on her spending, and the couple had terrible fights about what Rose was entitled to spend on herself from her family's estate. The more Marvin accepted Rose's demands and anger, the more disrespect she started to show toward him. Marvin started to keep his business life secret, and the two kept separate bank accounts.

By the time they came for therapy, there were years of resentment between them. Marvin complained that Rose would humiliate him in public, making him feel that he didn't know what he was talking about. Rose made all the financial decisions without consulting him, making him feel that "what's hers is hers, and what's mine is hers, too." Rose felt that she had been "taken in," just like her mother had been. She felt that her husband never put much energy into a job because he knew he would be taken care of, and she bitterly resented having to work and worry while he just kept on "humming." The more Marvin would try to keep the home light-hearted, the angrier Rose would become.

I asked Rose to think about what she had learned from her parents' marriage. Rose spoke easily about her father's gambling and expensive habits ruining the family's financial security, and realized that she had always believed that men weren't capable of much. She had grown up in a home where men always disappointed the women in their lives. It was hard for her to recognize Marvin's sincere efforts to succeed, and the painful feelings that he had about his own failures. Marvin's humor and easygoing attitude had been his way of not making the family miserable. Instead, Rose had concluded that he was unaffected by his own shortcomings, and would never become the partner she wished for. In her mind, her husband and father were the same, and she was hurt repeatedly in ways that were all too familiar.

Troubled Children

What is central to all of these couples is the underlying belief that in a marriage both partners cannot be simultaneously respected. Without ever challenging this idea, all of my clients had interpreted or reacted to their partners in a defensive way. Their parents' marriage had created expectations and beliefs about respect that restricted and complicated their ability to love and be loved safely.

Children are strongly affected when their parents demonstrate disrespect, whether the reactions are visible in their immediate behavior or in the years to come. If self-esteem is the foundation of well-being, then it is essential that spouses be able to treat each other in ways that build and reinforce respect. Each time a child watches one parent compliment the other, his own potential for self-esteem is enhanced. Each time he watches his parent give or accept unfair criticism or disapproval, his own expectations for a future of feeling valued are tarnished.

There will always be times when one spouse doesn't approve of what the other is doing. However, the way that disapproval is communicated should be carefully considered. I suggest that partners become responsible for curtailing comments that are disrespectful and wounding. Just as parents know that it is helpful to tell a child that something he has done is bad rather than communicate that *he* is bad, so partners can confine their criticism to specific issues. One problem that I frequently see in couples with distressed relationships is the devastating impact of generalizations and globalizations. A partner who is displeased has every right to express his feelings, but not in a way that condemns the other partner. Statements such as "You always" or "You never" escalate the situation and work against the desired outcome. The damage is compounded when little eyes and ears believe all this to be true.

There are many ways in which partners can demean each other. Sometimes the put-downs are couched in humor and are hard to identify as overt statements of disrespect. Parents also can choose to direct their comments to others, and share their marital miseries with friends or family. Unfortunately, few parents think about the harm that is done when children are listening to these "private" conversations. Perhaps the worst harm is done when one parent tells the children just how inadequate or terrible the other parent is.

When I work with families, I encourage partners to pay attention to their feelings. If they are feeling put down, they probably have been. I also help partners to gain the confidence they need to confront each other when this happens. For their own mental health and for the well-being of their children, parents must demand that they be treated with respect. Demanding respect does not mean refusing to listen to complaints or criticism, but it does mean insisting upon an approach that is not insulting or humiliating. I also encourage parents to tell each other when they like what their partner is doing, as it helps balance those moments when a criticism or complaint has dominated the emotional family atmosphere. Parents who value each other and themselves are able to show their children that marriage magnifies a person's worth, and that intimacy adds to personal well-being.

QUESTIONS

1. Would you say that one of your parents was smarter? More competent? More important? Which parent do you feel you are more like?

2. Would your children say that one of his or her parents is smarter? More competent? More important?

3. In general, do you feel good about yourself most of the time or is your self-confidence shaky?

4. Does your partner help you feel better about yourself or worse?

5. The worse thing partners can do to each other in terms of not showing respect is to _____. How often does this happen between you and your partner?

5
Maintaining Trust in Word and Deed

"Partners in a Marriage Try Not to Let Each Other Down"

PARENTS WHO IMAGINE A FUTURE in which their children can believe in and experience the goodness of others should not overlook the importance of maintaining trust in their marriage. While it is true that trust needs to be established in every successful relationship, it is an essential ingredient in intimacy. In order to develop a relationship where interdependency and honesty can be sustained, the couple must develop a mutual commitment to each other's well-being and happiness. Part of this comes from being able to assume goodwill and good intentions and the belief that partners will act to protect and to spare each other from emotional and physical harm. Trust also requires the expectation of a shared future where many of the goals of collective hard work will finally be realized. Because intimacy requires vulnerability, trust is essential if partners are to feel free to reveal themselves without the fear of being humiliated or rejected. Only trust makes it possible for partners to make substantial sacrifices, knowing that they are not being exploited and that there is reciprocity in the balance of give and take.[1] For all of these reasons, when trust is broken, the relationship and the legacy to the children are jeopardized.

There are many different situations that can test or rupture a couple's belief in commitment and mutual caretaking. I have worked with couples whose dilemmas were magnified because of differences in financial assets. I have also found that trust is easily tested when there are competing loyalties, such as in the case of blended families, where partners must balance their commitment to their children from a previous marriage with their devotion to a new partner. There are also unresolved issues around trust for adult children whose parents were divorced and for those who grew up in families where one or both parents were having affairs. While there is often some overlap, there are different dimensions of commitment that are being violated in each of these situations.

Commitment to Each Other's Well-Being

Falling in love generates a positive flow of warm and tender feelings. Because the gift of love is precious, partners want to take care of and protect each other from the pain and stress that others might inflict. But as vulnerable as a person is to their family or coworkers, they are more exposed to their partner and need to know that their partner will never turn on them in an emotionally abusive way. In order to develop trust, partners need to believe that they will be treated with respect and that their happiness will not be sabotaged.

When partners know that they are safe with each other, they can reveal dimensions of themselves that are very personal and sensitive. They can also engage in acts of kindness and love knowing that these acts will be reciprocated by the other. When children see these qualities in their parents, they can feel the safety and security of the marital bond. Parents who are committed to each other's well-being do not attack each other physically or verbally, and they display overall respect and concern. As a result, children learn that marriage is a place where people offer each other affection and support and help each other get through life's challenges.

This dimension of trust is based on the expectation that partners will value each other above all else. Unfortunately, there are certain conditions that challenge this assumption from the start. One area that I have encountered is the defensive posture created when one partner enters a marriage with strong financial assets. Because people are frequently exploited for their money, it is not uncommon for the wealthy partner to question his or her partner's motives from the beginning. "Am I genuinely loved for who I am, or for my money?" is the private, unsettling question. Often there is extensive testing to challenge the lover's "true" feelings and commitment. And, of course, before the wedding, the issue of a prenuptial agreement is inevitably raised.

While a legal document to protect an individual's wealth is probably necessary, the way that the agreement is presented and written can violate the less wealthy partner's sense of trust. Sometimes the precautions that are taken make the less wealthy partner feel like he or she is assumed to be a fortune hunter or is just in the relationship for the money. The division and separation of the money can lead to a division and separation of the sense of togetherness that underlies the partners' commitment to each other. Such was the case for Robin and Sam.

Robin and Sam

Robin originally contacted me for individual therapy, as she could not decide whether or not to end her dating relationship with

Sam. The couple had met at a gym and had struck up a conversation while running laps. For several weeks, their dating revolved around running dates followed by breakfast or dinner, and Robin enjoyed her new friend enormously. As the couple spent time together they discovered that beyond being physically alike, with lithe, athletic physiques, they had much in common. Each had been divorced previously, and each had two children from their previous marriages. In fact, their youngest daughters were only three weeks apart in age. Beyond that, they had traveled to some of the same countries, camped with their kids, and were passionate lovers of Broadway shows. When Sam finally took her home to his apartment one night, their sexual compatibility was confirmed, and the romance was in full bloom.

Sam had initially been evasive about his work, and simply explained that he was a lawyer. However, after a few months of regular dating, Robin discovered that Sam was actually a senior partner of a prestigious firm, and was, in fact, a millionaire. Sam seemed uncomfortable with Robin's "knowing," and peculiar kinds of fights started to happen. When Sam asked Robin to be his date for a business dinner, she blushed and explained that she didn't really own the kind of dress that would be appropriate for the fancy restaurant where it was being held. Sam joked about running up business expenses, and took Robin to the fanciest dress store in town. Robin told me that Sam seemed to enjoy helping her choose her new dress, but later, when they were in the car, he grew morose and said, "Don't think that I will buy all your clothes from now on." The thought had never occurred to Robin, and she felt hurt and insulted.

A few months later, Sam broached the subject of living together. Because of the children, the couple had not had much private time at night, and both were tired of trying to get difficult ex-spouses to switch their custodial schedules so that they could be alone together. On the one hand, Sam was very generous, offering to rearrange his apartment so that Robin and her children could be comfortable. But as the couple started to talk about the details, Robin again became anxious. Sam would grow stern and say, "Your children should not expect the same kind of things that my children get. Justin has a TV in his room, but I have no intention of buying one for Pam. And your kids better understand that some of the things in the family room are off-limits. Justin is very particular about his pool table; if he doesn't want your daughters to touch it, then that's his decision." Imagining a life where her children would be exposed to things that they couldn't touch or even dream of having made Robin uncomfortable. None the less, she figured the kids would work it out among themselves and agreed to the move.

The day that Robin called me for help was the day after Sam had told her he had no interest in getting married. Robin had expected that if things continued to go well, a wedding was part of the plan. If Sam was serious about his refusal to wed, then Robin had second thoughts about their living arrangement. Her daughters liked Sam's children, but the kids had not become as "tight" as Robin had wished. Her younger daughter, a slightly overweight and awkward nine-year-old, had become increasingly withdrawn, and often compared herself in a negative way to Sam's slim, athletic daughter. Her elder daughter had no interest in Justin's pool table, but found his possessiveness a bit "strange." As a result, she kept mainly to herself and her own circle of friends.

After hearing about the situation, I recommended that Robin bring Sam in for premarital counseling, and he surprised her by immediately agreeing. When I asked Sam to tell me about his family, I was saddened by the story he told. His father was an affluent dentist who had forced a comparatively modest lifestyle on his wife. To this day, she had no idea of the family wealth. Each year his father would give her a blank joint tax return and she would sign her name on the dotted line. According to Sam, his father ran the house and didn't consult his mother or treat her as his equal. Although his mother seemed to put up with her husband's condescending attitude, she would show her displeasure by rejecting every present he ever bought her. Sam's blueprint of a marriage was one in which partners could never please each other, and rarely gave praise or affirmation. Because Sam had never seen trust or sharing between his parents, his expectations surrounding intimacy were negative. To him, a partnership was potentially exploitative and dangerous.

Although Sam did not want to repeat his parents' marriage, he often assumed that Robin would take advantage of his wealth. His father had taught him to set firm limits, and had acted by the motto "If you give someone an inch, they will take a foot." Robin was also struggling to know what was right or wrong. Her parents' marriage was not one she wanted to repeat, as there had been domination and occasional violence. As a result, Robin tried to deny her angry feelings and be the perfect, sweet wife she wished her mother had been. However, Robin's temper was less controlled toward the children and she would often take out her frustrations on them.

Sam needed to work through his ambivalent feelings toward Robin—especially in the areas of concern that he had not disclosed to her. Skilled at business negotiations, Sam would often find himself groping to find the right word in his discussions with Robin. He would become easily enraged and would walk away before his anger took over. Robin also had difficulty in talking out her differences with Sam, as she could sense his underlying temper, and would back off before either of them might lash out in destructive ways.

In our first session, Robin told Sam that it would be foolish to think the fact that he was rich didn't appeal to her. "But," she told him, "instead of providing security and pleasure, it just seems to get in our way." Sam confessed that he always wondered whether any woman could love him for "just plain him," and how thrilled he had been when he had "fooled" Robin into not even guessing about his wealth. He also told Robin how bitter he was at the way his first marriage had ended and his ex-wife's constant attempts to extort money from him. "She has never lived up to one of her promises or agreements, and I don't think you would either."

Eventually Robin and Sam were able to talk through some of their differences more openly and felt more confident that they could negotiate successfully. Sam took a hard look at the beliefs he had formed about women from the way his father treated his mother. Slowly the relationship became more open and close. When Robin discovered that she was pregnant, Sam immediately proposed marriage, but three weeks before the wedding surprised Robin with a prenuptial agreement that left Robin confused and furious. Sam had presented a formula for alimony based on the number of years the couple stayed together. There was no plan for division of any assets the couple accumulated together. In an emergency session, Robin explained that once again she felt mistrusted and not really cared about. Robin tried to tell her husband-to-be that most couples feel connected in working toward a shared future, and that the prenuptial plan made Robin feel that she did not belong in his future. How could he expect her to have fun decorating a house with him or choosing a new car if the underlying assumption was that everything belonged to him?

The couple eventually came to a compromise about the prenuptial agreement, but Robin went through her wedding day feeling pessimistic. She felt that all their hard work in communicating to establish trust had gone out the window when Sam presented her with the prenuptial agreement. The fact that it had been delivered to her so late in the game also made her angry, as she believed that Sam was a shrewd businessman who had made a calculated decision to use time on his side in order to win complete protection. After their honeymoon, the couple returned to therapy, where Robin was able to talk about how sad she was that Sam's money had become an obstacle to their closeness. It took months before Sam was slowly able to recognize and take responsibility for the part of his reactions that came from his family's mistrust of outsiders as well as the anger that he had stored from his divorce settlement. When he was able to see Robin for who she was, and his marriage as an opportunity to create a different kind of life, it was possible for both to trust again.

Blended Families

When partners are single when they meet and marry, they are free to pledge themselves totally to each other's well-being. The arrival of children compromises this expectation, but at least both partners are loving and caring for a child they share. However, in blended families, partners arrive at the marriage with a preexisting relationship and a responsibility to their children. Although a partner can acknowledge the extent to which a parent's love for his or her children is normal and important, there is often tension between the new and the preexisting relationships. As long as partners feel that they are indispensable to each other, they will continue the process of building trust and commitment. But when partners believe that they come second to the children, they will not be able to develop the dependency that is necessary to create a mutually supportive and loving environment.[2] It would be foolish for a person to make him or herself vulnerable to a partner who is perceived as always giving, first and foremost, to the children from a previous marriage.

Unfortunately, the reactions of children to a "new" adult in the home often exacerbate this situation. Researchers of blended families have learned that most children resent their parents' new love interest, and often act out their displeasure. Sometimes, the reality of a parent's new relationship shatters the child's fantasy that the natural parents will one day reunite. At other times, the children have become accustomed to the close parent-child relationship that typically develops in a single-parent home and are not prepared to share their parent's time and love. In the worst-case scenario, a competition develops between the partner and the children, so that there is tension and discord in the blended relationship and a no-win tug of war for the parent/partner's attention and love. Should the partner lose in this battle, it is impossible to build further commitment. This is what happened in the Frank family.

THE FRANK FAMILY

When I first met Jennifer and Donald, they were deeply in love but nervous about their future together. Two years earlier, Jennifer's husband had shocked her by demanding a divorce. At first, Donald was a supportive coworker to whom she could confide her feelings, but eventually their friendship developed a sexual dimension and the couple fell madly in love. Donald had two grown children from a previous marriage but had no contact with them at all. At the time of his divorce, he had been young, immature, and irresponsible. His wife had left him because of his gambling and drinking, and Donald reflected that this was probably what he deserved. He liked children, but had many complicated feelings about having failed his first family. At this point in his life, he had no interest in being a father to anyone else's kids.

Jennifer's ex-husband was a possessive father who shared custody of their ten-year-old daughter, Martha, and had her alternate weekends and two days of the week. Jennifer assured Donald that Martha *had* an active father, and that he would not be expected to be a stepdad. However, as Donald, Martha, and Jennifer started to spend more time together, the tension and problems became immediately visible. Angry at her father's immediate remarriage to his lover, Martha was sarcastic and distant to Donald from the beginning. Donald, who had been raised in a strict Catholic family, was appalled that Martha was allowed to speak disrespectfully to him, but was even more aghast at the way she treated her mother. In our first session, Jennifer defensively admitted that perhaps she was a bit too lenient with Martha, but that Martha was always a precocious child who had entertained everyone with her wit. What Donald experienced as a "smart mouth" was explained by Jennifer as her daughter's intelligence, and when Donald complained that Martha was manipulative, Jennifer assured him that it was just her independent nature. It was clear that the two had very different expectations of what was appropriate for a ten-year-old. Jennifer was hurt by Donald's criticism even though she knew that there was some truth to his comments.

The couple had run out of ideas on how to coexist. Donald needed Jennifer to set clear expectations for Martha about acting polite and emphasized that it was as stressful to listen to the mother-daughter interactions as it was to find himself in an unhappy tête-à-tête with Martha. When Jennifer defended Martha, Donald felt totally unloved and unsupported. Martha seemed to sense her "victory" over Donald, and would constantly test the limits when her mother was not around. Donald lived for the weekends and evenings Martha spent with her father, and found himself making plans to do other things most of the time that Martha was staying with her mother.

In therapy, Donald was encouraged to form a direct relationship with Martha, not as a father but simply that of an adult to a child. Donald found that there was a side to Martha that he enjoyed, but that he would be consumed by guilt after he spent any pleasant time with her. How could he reconcile being a friend to this child when he had walked out on his own son and daughter years earlier? Therapy provided Donald with an opportunity to address some of his conflicts and feelings, and although his daughter refused to accept his phone call, he reestablished contact with his son.

Jennifer also needed to get in touch with feelings that were complicating the newly formed family's chance of succeeding. One important insight was her fear of losing her daughter's love. Whenever Martha did not get her way, she would threaten to move in permanently with her father, and Jennifer would panic.

Once this was openly examined, Jennifer started to feel more confident in setting limits. Jennifer also became aware of her tendency to protect Martha from what she perceived as Donald's becoming very stern and threatening. Although she knew that Donald was fair, and would never physically harm her daughter, she often found herself impulsively getting involved whenever she heard "that tone of voice." In therapy, Jennifer was able to identify her memories of how her father would speak "that way" to both her and her mother when he was starting to lose his temper. But in her childhood home, the tension would always escalate into open warfare and screaming matches. Once Jennifer learned to separate her reaction to Donald's stern voice from her memories of an explosive and often sadistic father, she could discipline herself to stay out of the middle. As long as Donald acted within their agreed-upon limits, Jennifer was able to stop jumping in to rescue her daughter. As Donald once stated, "I don't mind losing to a kid, and I don't mind that Jennifer loves her daughter. I just want to feel like I belong here, too, and that I can be respected even if I can't be accepted." Until Jennifer learned to stay out of the middle, the trust placed in her by Donald was in jeopardy.

Emotional Abuse

While it is almost understandable how an unhappy triangle can be established when money or previous children enter the "twosome," I have also worked with many couples who turn against each other because of psychological problems that are slow to surface. Over the years, I have worked with many couples who are "narcissistically vulnerable."[3] The word "narcissism" usually evokes an image of a person who is overly confident, but, in fact, the opposite is true. Many individuals who appear to have ample self-esteem and stability are actually emotionally insecure. Although these people can function in a state of apparent confidence, their sense of well-being is fragile and easily broken. If a person with narcissistic vulnerability is criticized or made to feel inadequate, he or she will plummet from an "all-good" state into the "all-bad" sphere of feeling worthless. Because the "all-bad" state stimulates severe depression, anxiety, and discomfort, the narcissistically vulnerable person attempts to avoid it at all cost, and goes through life seeking praise or reassurance that will protect him. Unable to maintain the facade of confidence when he is criticized, his only alternative is to attack the person he believes is causing the injury. If he is able to humiliate this person into a state of feeling worthless, or if he can prove his superiority through powerful rage, he can rid himself of the threat of being swept into the "bad" state. Unfortunately, the person who most frequently is the target of his devaluing and rage is his partner.

In this kind of marriage it is not uncommon for partners to be unable to listen or respond to attempts to raise issues of difference for discussion. Problems are experienced as blame or criticism, which the narcissistically vulnerable person cannot tolerate. Envy is also easily stimulated, and even though the narcissistically vulnerable person might celebrate his partner's success, there is often a simultaneous effort to spoil the event or bring the partner down in a different way. A person who is narcissistically vulnerable might also do things to make his or her partner feel shamed or inadequate, as this frees him or her from experiencing these feelings firsthand.

I call this kind of relationship the roller-coaster marriage, as things tend to quickly go from great to terrible. Most of the individuals who live with narcissistically vulnerable partners hate the lack of stability and predictability in their lives, and complain that they are often emotionally abused. Being the victim of narcissistic rage, or having a partner who spoils a celebration, is indeed difficult to tolerate. Spouses tell me that they have to walk on eggshells to avoid another outburst or down cycle. They also talk to me about how discouraging it is when they realize that their complaints or ideas for improving the relationship will never be accepted or even honestly listened to. When a partner feels that his or her well-being always comes second, and that there are underlying currents of competition, resentment, or envy, then it is almost impossible to maintain trust. The fabric of intimacy cannot endure the levels of rage and insensitivity that are released in an episode that is emotionally abusive, and the first thread to tear is the partner's ability to trust that it will never happen again. If a cycle of "good" and "bad" gets established, the couple rarely returns to a state of closeness that is only possible when trust exists.

Children from these marriages watch their parents go through cycles of ups and downs, never fully understanding what makes a marriage happy or unhappy. They also hear their parents blame each other when things go wrong, and experience the extreme pessimism or rage that can take over the family when this happens. They will also often join the roller-coaster ride, trying to be good enough so that their behavior will not cause their parents to turn against each other again. It is not surprising that children from these marriages often appear to be compliant and perfect, but because of their ultimate powerlessness and failure to keep the family stable, they develop self-doubt. Rather than learn how partners can give each other support and comfort, these children watch parents turn into ferocious adversaries or distant strangers when there are problems. Just as the cycles of good and bad are frustrating and exhausting for the partners, the sudden appearance of severe marital discord and distancing creates confusion for the child. Because there are no examples of constructive conflict resolution, the child often gets the message that problems can be overwhelming and totally destructive. Above all, they see that when things get difficult, people are basically on their own.

Lies

Part of the formula for commitment to each other's well-being is truthfulness. Because the activities and feelings of one partner almost always affect the other, it is important to believe that there is easy access to information about areas of shared concern. This does not negate the right for personal privacy, but it does mean that there needs to be honesty about the things that affect both. When one partner lies to the other, the conditions upon which trust is built crumble. The lying partner must remain vigilant in order to preserve the lie and, in so doing, brings a sense of secrecy and tension to communication. The partner who feels deceived is often made anxious and furious by the lack of "knowing," which is often experienced as a feeling of being controlled or manipulated.

There are many reasons for why one partner might lie to the other. Deceit is almost always present in addictions, whether it be to alcohol, gambling, or sex. Extramarital affairs will rarely be carried out in total honesty, and the adulterer almost always has to lie about his or her whereabouts. Lies breed other lies, which become almost impossible to conceal. Once a partner discovers that he or she is being lied to, there is a desperate attempt to regain control and to know "everything." In an attempt to "find out the truth," the partner might become obsessed with watching and cross-examining the lying partner, a situation that almost always leads to battles over control.[4] It is a no-win situation for the partners and for the children, who can see the amount of suspicion and mistrust that exists between their parents. Of course the situation is exacerbated if one parent confides in the child and tries to pressure the child into maintaining the secret. A child might also be triangled into the parents' control struggles by being asked to "report" what they know about a given situation. Parents who involve their children in the lie or in the pursuit of truth teach them that basically no one can be trusted. Partners are not friends who respect and do their best to help each other; they are opponents who might cheat and resort to unethical behavior in their quest to be free from each other's influence.

Violation of a Partner's Needs

Trust is established by actions that verify each partner's respect for the other's feelings and needs. While there are always differences in what partners want or how they think things should be carried out, partners have to trust that their spouse would never purposefully do something that violates what the partner feels strongly about. A partner who disregards his or her partner's position on an important subject is sending a message of disrespect. When this happens, partners turn against each other in a struggle for control instead of working together to find a compromise or a balance. Whether the violation occurs with open defiance or passive innocence, the result is still a breach of trust.

I have known couples who have hurt each other in this way when dealing with punctuality, where one person's need to be on time was met with her partner's response of dawdling and getting involved in last-minute projects that made him perpetually late. Many couples engage in struggles around spending and become embroiled in issues that involve money. One couple I worked with had constant arguments about the wife's overspending, which her husband felt was an addiction. The more her husband begged her to stop spending, the more bargain buys she would come home with. Although the husband had a secure job, he was committed to saving for his three children's college educations and for his eventual retirement. Debt made him highly anxious, and dipping into the savings account to pay for his wife's new wardrobe made him feel unloved and violated. When couples are constantly bickering like this, the children cannot help but know. Marriage seems like a tug of war between opponents, with only one player winning.

When parents cannot respect or work through their differences around the way their children are raised, the results are even more devastating. It is one thing when parenting issues arise that neither parent is fully prepared for. Parents often have different ideas or strategies, and may pressure their partner to agree to their plan. But when parents have discussed an issue fully and have arrived at a clear position, then their partner's sabotage is felt as an act of betrayal. The children become pawns in their parents' power struggle, aware of the competing positions and caught in the middle. The Kleins were a family that struggled in this way for years.

THE KLEIN FAMILY

Saul Klein was the only son in a devoutly religious family. He never directly confronted his parents' attempts to force their religious commitment on him, but he somehow fell in love with a Catholic woman in college. His parents were devastated but Saul and Marie decided to marry anyway. Marie agreed to convert to Judaism and raise their children in the Jewish faith. While the Jewish religious observations were not uncomfortable for her, she deeply missed the Christmas celebrations that her family enjoyed every year. The couple compromised, agreeing that Marie would be able to go home every December and share in this family event that held so much meaning for her.

Problems did not surface until they had children. Marie had not joined her family for Christmas when the twins were very young, and had even agreed to send the boys to a Jewish nursery school. However, when the twins were three, Marie decided that she was going home for Christmas, and insisted that the children join her to visit their grandparents and the rest of her family. Saul felt that this would create too much confusion for them, but Marie bought airplane tickets for the whole family. At the last minute, Saul decided that he could not join his family for business reasons. The children came home excited with the presents they had received Christmas morning and with stories of the wonderful tree they had helped decorate. Saul felt betrayed at what he felt was Marie's attempt to convert his children to Catholicism, and the two began to fight bitterly. Saul insisted that involving the children in the celebration of Christmas was a violation of Marie's promise to raise Jewish children, and felt that he could not trust that she would honor the vows she had made before their marriage. It took months of each trying to understand a very different view of the meaning of Christmas before trust could be reestablished.

Commitment to Sexual and Emotional Exclusivity

Although different cultures have permitted sexual activity outside the marital relationship, most people who get married in our country today have an expectation of sexual exclusivity. Because marriage is a product of love, it is assumed that romantic involvement occurs between the marital partners, and that turning to a different partner would cause hurt for the left-out spouse. Most couples demand sexual exclusivity from each other at some point during their dating, and there are often issues of jealousy that need to be worked through until trust is developed.

However, the reality is that a very large number of married people do have extramarital affairs. In a recent study of men over the age of fifty, more than one half had been involved in at least one affair.[5] While this might reflect the behavior of men who spent their early married days in an era during which the belief that "boys will be boys" was more prevalent, estimates on the sexual fidelity of today's parents have not changed that much. And so it seems that many of today's families are living with the consequences of infidelity—either as a grown child who may still be reacting to the experience of growing up in a home disrupted by adultery, or as parents who are struggling with the impact of an affair on their own relationship and on their children.

The Effect on Children

As I have suggested throughout this book, children are much more aware of their parents' relationship than parents would like to believe. When trust is secure in a marriage, there is little tension or suspicion about each partner's whereabouts or activities. Because there are no secrets, communication is open and relaxed. Children from these marriages can afford to be less focused on the meaning and consequences of their parents' behavior, as their vigilance is not needed to preserve family harmony.

In contrast, children whose parents are involved in extramarital affairs are aware of the tension, secrecy, and distance between their parents. Once the affair has been discovered, things usually get much worse. Loyalty conflicts almost always occur as each parent tries to elicit support for his or her position. Often, the parent who has been cheated on may try to poison the children's feelings toward the unfaithful partner. As a result, the child may be given a great deal of information that is age inappropriate and damaging to hear. Even though adolescents are old enough to know about sex, they are in a delicate stage of forming their own moral standards, and often feel betrayed and offended by a parent's adultery. Children of all ages recognize the seriousness of the situation and become anxious. As psychologist Emily Brown suggests, the child makes an immediate leap from the awareness of an affair, which is an indirect experience, to the expectation of an impending divorce, which will affect the child firsthand. Unfortunately, neither parent can assure the child that a divorce will not happen, and when children cannot be given this reassurance, they usually anticipate the worst.[6]

The children who are most damaged by infidelity are the ones who are triangled into their parents' problem. Although the parents may have been drifting apart for a long time, the discovery of an affair punctuates the seriousness of the marital problems and the potential for permanent rupture. Each parent may attempt to win the loyalty of their children, which necessarily pits them against the other parent. Parents may turn inappropriately to their children to get support, fully disclosing the details of their marital situation and permanently carving the presence of the third party into the family's life. When a parent becomes aware of his or her partner's attempts to win the children's loyalties, the rift between the parents usually intensifies. It is as if each parent is desperately trying to hold on to and preserve something of value in his or her life: "You have destroyed my trust and my hope in our future together. You will never take my children away from me."

Children are often left angry at both parents. Because affairs may happen in marriages that seem perfect on the surface, the children may not suspect that their parent is capable of such immoral or deceitful behavior. As Brown points out, the discovery of an affair blows the perfect parent off his or her pedestal. However, the unknowing parent usually has a hard time adjusting to the reality of the infidelity. Often, the cheating spouse does not want to end the marriage but also does not want to give up the lover. This is an excruciating situation for the wronged partner, who feels powerless and afraid to express his or her rage out of fear that it might tip the balance toward the lover. Should the wronged parent become depressed or emotionally overwhelmed, some children will also get frustrated and will eventually become angry. "Deal with it and stop moping" is the advice of a teenager, to whom a broken romance is part of the process of inevitable change. Other children will become sympathetic and caretaking. In either case, the child's days of innocence are over.

It is always more difficult when the child is the one who discovers the affair. In some situations, a parent may confide in a child, hoping for some form of reassurance and permission. This puts a terrible burden on a child, who is forced to conceal a secret from the other parent and thus becomes a complicit partner in the deception. When a father turns to a son for acceptance of his adulterous activities, he often approaches the subject as an initiation into the "real" world of men. In so doing, he provides his son with a clear statement about the unimportance of sexual exclusivity and attempts to influence his son's developing beliefs about relationships with women. In one family I knew, the father took his teenage son to bars with him, and openly shared stories about different women with whom he had recently been sexually involved. His message to his son was that it is a man's right to find pleasure for himself and not be ruled by a woman. His defiance against his wife and open disrespect for her were clearly communicated. Not surprisingly, the young man began his own acts of infidelity within two months of his honeymoon.

Children can also be the first to learn about the affair from clues that are carelessly disclosed or that are accidentally discovered. The child must then declare a loyalty by choosing to keep or to tell the secret. Often, the position of disclosing the secret to the unknowing parent creates an immediate coalition between parent and child, as the child is exposed to the shock, disbelief, and pain that usually accompanies first hearing about the affair. In a moment of great emotional distress, the parent may not even think twice about unburdening his or her own feelings on the child. Knowing that one parent has caused such hurt to the other adds to the child's sense of injustice and usually impairs the child's relationship with the adulterous parent. This is what happened in the Glenn family.

THE GLENN FAMILY

Amanda, age ten, learned about her father's affair quite innocently. When she went to make a phone call one day, her father was talking to someone on the extension. Something that was said caught her attention, and she stayed on the line undetected. Within minutes she heard her father, Daniel, joke about how his wife had no idea about last night's dinner escapade. Comments were made about how great the after-dessert sex had been, at which point Amanda quietly set the phone back on the hook.

For the rest of the day Amanda was unable to look at either of her parents. Her normally cheerful mood evaporated and she spent the day in her room. Finally she went to her mother and started to cry. She told her mother the details of the overheard conversation, and both cried together. Margaret had known about an earlier affair and had threatened to divorce Daniel if it ever happened again. Without thinking, she told her daughter everything, not masking her rage and pain. Amanda held her mother's hand and told her that she would stand by her no matter what happened. Only then did Margaret stop to think about the effect of all this on her daughter.

When Margaret confronted Daniel, he did not attempt to cover up his affair but once again pleaded with Margaret not to pursue a divorce. Frustrated by Margaret's decision to stand by her earlier threat, he turned to Amanda. "I made a mistake, but I really want our family to stay together. Your mom is so stubborn. She just won't forgive me no matter how hard I beg. Believe me, the last thing I want is a divorce."

Now Amanda was completely split. On the one hand, she wished her mother would back down so that the family could stay together. At the same time, she had seen how hurt her mother was, and knew that her mom needed her support to get through this situation. It took family therapy to get the parents to realize the devastating toll this competition was having on their daughter, and learn to leave her out of it.

THE EFFECT ON GROWN CHILDREN

A family ruptured by a parent's infidelity does not always survive. Current research suggests that half of the couples end up divorcing, and that this is more likely to happen if the unfaithful spouse is the wife or if the husband has had previous affairs. Although many unfaithful women stay involved with their lovers, only 10 percent of all people who divorce because of an affair marry the lover.[7] It is hard, then, to really know what hurts children the most: living through the secrecy and tension before the affair is made public, enduring the emotional chaos after the disclosure of the affair, going through their parents' divorce, or, in some cases, having to form a relationship with a stepparent who "broke up" their parents' marriage. For some or all of these reasons, a parent's affair has a strong impact on the children, and continues to affect their relationships and ability to trust well into adulthood.

Psychologist Judith Wallerstein, who studied children for ten years after their parents' divorce, discovered that the grown children whose parents divorced because of an affair were still "intensely preoccupied with a parent's infidelity."[8] Other studies show that college students whose parents divorced after an infidelity had difficulty in trusting their dating partners, and were often cynical or pessimistic about love. Even more surprising to me is the fact that adult children whose parents had affairs are more likely than other people to be unfaithful to their partners.[9] Once again, the blueprint of the parents' marriage surfaces and creates a defensive posture or a duplication. One couple who had major problems as a result of this was Kirt and Sandra.

KIRT AND SANDRA

Kirt and Sandra had been married for less than a year when they started marriage therapy. Sandra had worked as Kirt's secretary for eight years, and the couple had begun their affair three years before they married. Kirt was unhappily married but was committed to the well-being of his three children. When his youngest daughter turned thirteen, Kirt felt that the kids were sufficiently involved in their own lives to not be too disrupted by a divorce, and he told his wife that he was in love with another woman.

Kirt's wife, Maggie, was devastated and enraged, and did her best to turn the children against their father. She was especially distraught that Kirt and Sandra established a home together immediately, and that Sandra participated in all the children's visits. At their mother's urging, they requested private time with their dad, but Sandra refused to be left out. The children knew that their father had left the family to be with Sandra, and rejected her attempts at friendship. The truth was that Sandra knew exactly how they felt. When she was fourteen, her father had left home to be with his mistress, and her mother had never fully recovered. Sandra had also felt jealous and left out when she went to visit her dad, a situation that was made considerably worse after her half-sister was born.

Soon the couple started to fight during and after the children's visits. Sandra demanded that Kirt stand up for her and not allow the children to speak to her disrespectfully. Although Kirt did intervene when the kids were cold or rude, many times he felt that Sandra was too sensitive. "You're expecting too much from them. Just give it some time and they will realize that you're not the monster Maggie makes you out to be."

As the months wore on, Sandra became more intolerant of Kirt's lack of awareness and support for her position. Kirt and his best friend had shared basketball tickets for fifteen years. This season it was Sandra, not Maggie, who accompanied Kirt to the opening game. Sandra felt that she had been scrutinized by almost everyone at that game, and that people were staring at her and gossiping about the "scandal." What especially hurt Sandra was Kirt's getting involved in enjoying the game, leaving her to try to make small talk with a woman who had been one of Maggie's closest friends. When Kirt told Sandra she was making too much of it, she withdrew and smoldered for days.

In therapy, I was interested in hearing about Sandra's memories of her parents' marriage and how she had handled her father's affair. Sandra had been her father's favorite child, and she had long been aware that her father had no respect for or interest in her mother. Thus, when Sandra found out about her dad's affair, she felt that *she* had been betrayed. In her eyes, her father loved her more than he did her mother. When her dad moved out to be with another woman, Sandra felt crushed and rejected. She was angry that her mother never really got her life together again, and resented her mother's depressions and attempts to get closer to her daughter. Sandra fantasized about moving in with her dad, but quickly changed her mind when she learned her father and his new wife were having a baby. Sandra had vowed never again to be powerless or dependent.

During one of the sessions, I was talking to Kirt about his tendency to minimize Sandra's feelings, and wondered if he did the same with his own. Something resonated deep within Kirt, and he started to cry as he talked about never trusting that his feelings would be cared about. To my surprise, when Kirt had finished talking, Sandra exploded. Barely able to control her rage, she screamed at Kirt that he had never even tried to talk to her about his most important feelings—let alone cry. At that point, I realized that Sandra was also furious with me, furious and jealous. The next week the couple canceled their appointment. Kirt apologized when I called their home, and explained that Sandra was feeling uncomfortable in the sessions. He reassured me that some of my suggestions had been very helpful, but that he could not force Sandra to continue if the sessions were going to make her so upset. Only then did I fully realize the extent to which Sandra's parents' marriage had affected her. Unable to trust in any man's faithfulness, she could not tolerate Kirt's affection for his children or for his friends. Kirt's opening up to a female therapist had made Sandra feel inadequate and anxious. Her fear of losing yet another man made her pressure Kirt into con-

stantly proving his devotion to her, and walking away from any relationships that threatened her. Kirt had lost his therapist, and was on
the road to losing his children as well.

GOOD OUTCOMES

There is one note of optimism: Sometimes an affair helps partners to recognize and deal with problems that have simmered
under the surface for years. Of the 50 percent of marriages in
which divorce did not occur, a good number of couples learned to
recognize their masked conflict and handle their differences and
problems directly. When parents are able to use an affair as information to correct and restore their marriage, then the children
learn that if trust is reestablished, partners can get through the
worst of times and come out ahead. The children are left with a
much better model for problem solving and a belief in the good
that can come from not giving up.

Surviving Divorce

Despite the fact that over half the children in America will experience their parents' divorce, most Americans still believe in marriage as the ideal way in which people should live their lives.[10] "Till
death do us part" seals the typical marriage vows, and silver and
golden anniversaries are celebrated. When divorce enters the picture, the children are always affected: in the aftermath of the family's rupture, and in subsequent years when they must grapple with
their own ability to commit to love for life. Although children of
divorced parents no longer feel the stigma that they might have
experienced fifteen or twenty years ago, they still describe their parents' divorce as a stressful and unhappy time that they will never
forget.

Understanding the impact of divorce on a child is not easy, for there are three things that may be happening concurrently. First, many divorces occur because of infidelity, and the child is affected by all of the factors that were discussed above. Second, many divorces follow years of destructive marital conflict. Exposure to chronic conflict, whether it be cold wars or screaming matches, leads to serious psychological harm in children (see Chapter Seven). And finally, divorce between the parents often translates into divorce between one parent and the children, as many children lose contact and emotional connection with the noncustodial parent.[11] The loss of this relationship is believed to be more devastating than the end of the family structure as the child has known it, with two parents and the kids living under the same roof.

EFFECTS ON GROWN CHILDREN

When adults describe the effect of their parents' divorce, there seem to be two opposite kinds of reactions. At one end are the people who seem suspicious and mistrustful of commitment, who are cautious about the likelihood of their own marriage succeeding. College students whose parents were divorced agreed with the statement "There are few good or happy marriages these days," while their counterparts from intact families disagreed. In another study, 82 percent of college students whose parents had divorced said that they did not fully trust their current dating partner. Many said that they purposefully tested and broke off relationships, stating that they "would rather be the one to leave than be left." The fear of being abandoned or betrayed is particularly common among young adult women whose parents divorced after the discovery of an affair.[12] The way that trust was broken in their parents' marriage seems to dangle as a curse on their own right to happiness.

However, there is another group of grown children who believe strongly in marital commitment. People who fall into this category stress the importance of trust and permanence in marriage and are determined not to be like their parents. This seems to be an example of disidentification, as the children devote themselves to honoring their marriage vows in a way their parents failed to do. One young man I heard about used his grandfather's wedding band in his wedding ceremony as a tribute to and identification with his grandfather's happy, intact marriage.[13]

One goal that grown children of divorce seem to share is a desire to protect their children. Many describe themselves as being "overprotective," and make a point of letting their children be children.[14] For these parents, the memories of emotionally caring for their own parents and growing up too quickly have left permanent scars. They also talk about missing out on attention, and try to give that to their own children. Not surprisingly, many of the mothers speak about feeling more comfortable in their role of mother than in their role of wife, especially when the divorce took place when they were young and they have few memories of their parents' marriage. The consequences of growing up in a family without a marriage is not completely clear, as many individuals whose parents divorced when they were young are able to create fulfilling partnerships. But for others, there are difficulties in maintaining long-term relationships. Both men and women from divorced families have the highest divorce rates in their own marriages.[15] Several studies have focused on the attitudes and relationship experiences of African Americans, who are three times as likely to be raised in female-headed households. In many of these families, the parental bonds had been broken, so mothers were left to manage on their own. Although these women tend to develop and rely on relationships with friends and family, there seem to be both positive and negative consequences. African-American women are less likely to wait to have children until they are married; a recent census showed that almost 70 percent had their first child out of wedlock. They are also twice as likely to leave a marriage when things are not working out, regardless of the number of children or the children's ages.[16]

This does not mean to imply that African Americans are not able to develop successful long-term marriages. There are many studies of successful long-term marriages that include African-American couples who were very invested in their marriages. However, many of these partners come from intact families.[17] This seems to suggest that when children see their parents depend on each other and give each other support, they are better able to make a long-standing commitment to marriage. Children who grow up in a family without a strong parental bond seem to have less need for marriage and are less likely to persevere when serious problems arise.

Making Divorce Work

There is a lot of research on children of divorce that can help parents going through this help their children make the best possible adjustment. Children do best when the divorce is amicable, or at least minimally conflictual. When children are not exposed to extreme fighting and when they are not used as pawns for revenge or control, their adjustments are relatively smooth. Children who feel "caught" between their parents because they have been drawn into the conflict or have been used in a loyalty tug of war are deeply affected and are likely to suffer from problems that include headaches, eating disorders, anxiety, and depression.[18]

Another critical factor is being able to stay close to both parents after the physical separation. For reasons that are not entirely understood, fathers tend to withdraw from their children when they are not the custodial parent. Some researchers speculate that fathers give up when they feel they have no real say or control over what is happening in their children's lives; others speculate that the loss of the separation is just too emotionally difficult for fathers to live with on a daily basis, and that distance allows them to escape from overwhelming feelings. Regardless of the cause, almost half of the children of divorce haven't seen their noncustodial parent (usually the father) in the past year, and only one in six has weekly contact.[19]

Children do not cope well with this loss while it is happening, and appear to be permanantly injured by what they experience as abandonment. The need for fathers to stay connected to their children throughout the divorce process, and after, simply cannot be overstated.

What happens to each parent after the divorce is equally important. Children who do the best have parents who either remain single or become involved in a stable, successful relationship. In contrast, children whose parents have subsequent divorces or who change partners frequently have the highest incidence of emotional problems and difficulty in establishing trust in their own relationships.

Kids don't ask for the divorce, and seldom benefit from it. Parents can make the best of a bad situation by remembering to put the children first in as many ways as they can. When children are protected from direct exposure to their parents' anguish and hostility, they seem to do much better. By focusing on becoming an effective co-parent and keeping the children out of the middle of a failed relationship, a divorced parent can take positive steps to minimize long-term harm to the children. A parent's bitterness cannot help but erode a child's dreams and take away the hope of his or her own happy marriage. A parent who remains suspicious and self-protective after a divorce confirms the belief that people should not be trusted and that it is foolish to hope for something different.

Trust is one component of a marriage that is barely thought about when it is in place, but is totally consuming when it is broken. Partners who lie, manipulate, or violate a commitment cause immediate harm to a relationship, which must be addressed in order to be healed. Situations that test commitment always put trust in jeopardy, for when a spouse is not assured of his or her partner's devotion, there is no reason to justify the self-sacrifices that are needed to make a marriage work. When children grow up in a marriage where trust is a given, there is no tension or suspicion to force them into vigilance. Open communication and confidence are theirs to see and emulate. But when children discover that partners are secretive, self-serving, and manipulative, it is much harder for them to hope for a future that will be different.

QUESTIONS

1. To what degree do you think you were motivated to find an intimate relationship when you were a young adult? Did your parents' marriage serve as an inspiration for this?

2. Did either of your parents have an affair? Divorce? Remarry? How do you think your beliefs and expectations about marriage were affected by this?

3. Was there ever a time when you doubted your partner's commitment to the marriage or to your well-being? If so, was it thoroughly discussed and responded to, or are there leftover doubts?

4. How often have you or your partner threatened to divorce or separate? Do you think your children are aware of this?

6

Negotiating Differences Constructively

"Sometimes We Disagree, but We Always Stick with It and Work It Out"

O F ALL THE LESSONS that parents unknowingly teach their children, perhaps the one that has the most visible consequences is how parents handle their differences. In the fantasy of a shared life, partners smile and hold hands as they walk together in total harmony. In the reality of a shared life, there are always moments when what one partner sees or wants is different from what the other partner sees or wants. Because sharing a life means that the actions of one person always affect the other, every couple must find a way to make joint decisions and learn to accept the influence of their partner.

Knowing how to negotiate, how to assert oneself without diminishing one's partner, and how to compromise without resentment are key ingredients for success, but they are skills that need to be learned, practiced, and fine-tuned. When parents have different approaches or opinions, the children are acutely aware of the tensions that exist. And the way in which parents handle themselves and treat each other teaches children the basics of problem resolution and power.

While most people are aware that certain kinds of parental conflict are harmful for the children, many parents do not understand the problems that are created when they are afraid to assert themselves and instead avoid conflict altogether. Researchers of marital therapy have found that couples who rarely disagree are the first to become distant and unhappy.[1] The absence of conflict does not mean that two people are always in sync, but more likely indicates that for one reason or another spouses are afraid to disagree. Partners in this kind of environment grow resentful and detached. Children who are raised in this environment often get too involved in their parents' marriage, either by replacing one parent as the source of intimate contact or by acting as a go-between. Beyond that, they never have the opportunity to witness how differences can be handled constructively.

Fear of Feelings

I have found that one of the principle reasons parents avoid conflict is because they do not know how to manage their feelings. Many of my clients have grown up in family environments where feelings were not tolerated, and they have never learned how to decipher their inner states. Some parents are able to offer their children comfort when they are upset, but do not know how to teach their children to find the words that express their emotional turbulence. Learning how to put feelings into words takes patience and a parent who is willing to listen to and confirm the child's inner experiences. If parents are not able to help their children with this process, it is unlikely that the children will learn to do it on their own. Instead, they learn to ignore their feelings, distract themselves, or find an outlet that allows release without insight.[2]

While these ways of managing feelings may help an adult successfully cope with some stressful situations, they will not prepare a person to respond to the kinds of problems that are typically encountered in intimate relationships. And unless a person takes the time to stay with uncomfortable feelings until she understands her own emotional state, she will not be able to talk to her spouse about the things that are bothering her. She may distract herself or try to forget about her problem, but the feelings will continue and usually become deeper. When the differences are finally acknowledged, they are so enormous that they seem insurmountable. This is what happened to Randi and Adam.

RANDI AND ADAM

Randi called me in tears, saying that Adam had asked for a separation and that she was completely beside herself. The couple had been married for twenty years, and Randi had thought that everything was fine. Their eldest daughter was leaving for college in the fall, and their sixteen-year-old son was old enough to take care of himself if the couple wanted to go away for the weekend. The summer plans of family barbecues and a trip to the shore were suddenly up in smoke.

Adam admitted that he was attracted to another woman at work, and that one of the reasons he wanted to move out was so that he could date her without feeling guilty or secretive. However, he agreed to go to marital counseling once he had set himself up in his own apartment. Randi was in tears throughout the appointment, but challenged Adam's sudden decision. She felt as if she had been blindsided, and had no idea what Adam was unhappy about.

Adam said that home was where his clothes and books were, but that he felt detached from both Randi and the kids. Their son, Brian, was causing Adam considerable frustration, and he found himself dreading the commute home after work. Saying "I love you" to Randi had become a meaningless phrase, and he simply didn't want to continue what he felt was a pretense. Even though the couple told me that they never fought, Adam was visibly upset and agitated as he started to list the things that were wrong with Brian. Brian was unkempt, had terrible manners, was totally irresponsible, and assumed that he could sleep the day away and be provided with money to drive the car around at night. Adam couldn't stand the way Brian was turning out, and the way that Randi sabotaged every attempt he made to set or enforce standards.

Their different expectations for the children had been evident from the beginning. Adam admitted that when the children were very young he had often deferred to Randi, since she was the one spending the most time with the kids and because she seemed so certain that her way was best. But as the children grew older, Adam became more upset with Randi's lax, permissive approach. In his opinion, both children had Randi completely wrapped around their fingers. But whereas their daughter, Phoebe, had seemed to have more common sense and had been blessed by the influence of a good circle of friends, Brian took advantage of his mother's kindness at every opportunity. As a result, he had failing grades in several subjects, and had no plans for summer school or a summer job.

Even though Randi and Adam agreeably answered my questions about how they had met and the early days of their marriage, they were baffled when I told them I wanted to get some information about their childhood families. They agreed to the detour after I explained that I was interested for two reasons: It was apparent that they had different values and expectations for their children that I wanted to know more about, and, of even more importance, I needed to understand how a problem of this magnitude could have simmered for years in a couple who agreed that they never fought.

As I expected, the lifestyles of the two families were almost completely opposite. Adam's family valued education and demanded that their children work hard and achieve top grades. Randi couldn't remember her parents ever placing an expectation on her. In some ways, she thought that her mother would have preferred it if she had stayed at home and simply been her friend. Where Adam had to put himself through school and help with his share of the household responsibilities, Randi had always gone to summer camp, and was only allowed to baby-sit occasionally. Most of all, Adam's family had stressed accountability, and the responsibility of every family member to achieve the highest goals possible. In contrast, Randi's family was relatively easygoing and had rarely challenged her decisions to experiment with and then drop out of different sports, music lessons, or courses.

Their parents' marriages, however, were not that very different. Adam's mother was a powerful, successful woman who ended up taking over her husband's business after he had failed with it. Adam said, "Mom ran the house. She was the one we always had to answer to." Adam's parents would fight, but his father would always give in. However, Adam was sure that his dad had a private life that was beyond his mother's control. When I asked him to explain this for me, Adam sheepishly replied, "I know that he had at least one affair."

In Randi's family, it had been her father who ran the house. Randi's dad had a terrible temper and dominated his wife and children. He would shout and his wife would back down. But Adam interrupted to say, "She would look like she had backed down. And then, when he wasn't looking, she'd do exactly what she wanted to. And that's what you have always done to me, too."

Neither Randi nor Adam had grown up in a home where the parents could talk out their differences in a respectful way or work with each other toward a solution. In response to an angry, controlling partner, one of the parents had developed a style of passively avoiding conflict but at the same time refusing to be dominated. For the twenty years of their marriage, both Randi and Adam were uncomfortable with their feelings of anger and coped with differences by changing the subject or making a joke. Adam spent most of his time at work or on the golf course and rarely raised confrontational issues. Now, when so many aspects of his life at home felt unbearable, Adam's only solution was to bail out. In his fantasy, a new lover could be more like him, and if there were fewer differences he would never feel distressed. Only when Adam realized that the real issue was learning to stand up and fight constructively for what was important could he recommit to working on keeping his marriage intact.

Talking about Brian made Adam experience the full force of his feelings of powerlessness, resentment, and despair. But by staying with the issue, Randi and Adam were better able to sort out the situation and put things in perspective. Adam realized that he was not only afraid of the anger he felt toward Randi, but that he also had great difficulty in acknowledging and expressing his feelings directly to Brian. In some ways, it was easier to avoid a direct confrontation and then put the blame on Randi. Randi also needed to examine the relationship she had developed with her son, and how she had never dealt with her own feelings or confronted her husband about his absence and his critical stance. It did not take Randi long to realize that Brian made her feel needed and important, an emotional experience that she had never had with her husband. Only then could the couple begin to correct the loneliness each felt and try to be more responsive to each other.

Therapy involved creating a direct relationship between Brian and his father, one that Randi could not be held responsible for. Father and son spent a weekend together skiing, and basically trying to get to know each other and have some fun. When Adam was eventually able to tell Brian how disappointed and frustrated he felt, Brian, in turn, was able to express his own feelings of feeling unloved and inadequate. By getting things out in the open, everyone in the family experienced the relief that honesty can bring, and the hope that differences could be worked with instead of denied.

Marriages of the Children of Alcoholics

It is estimated that over 40 percent of today's families have one parent who grew up in a home where alcohol or another addiction influenced family relationships.[3] Because every child accepts the family's style of relating as normal, and the parents' marriage as the prototype for all intimate relationships, the lessons learned in these homes are affecting the lives of thousands of parents and children—even though alcohol or drugs may be banned from the home! Addiction compromises every aspect of a person's life, including how well he or she can function as a partner or a parent. As a result, family roles must shift, which places immediate stress on children who may either be given too much responsibility or are left too much on their own. But alcohol influences the family in other ways and introduces lessons of relating that contradict what children really need to learn. High on the list of dysfunctional lessons is the silencing of feelings and the denial of individual needs.

Experts on alcoholic families feel that it is not the drunken behavior alone that creates psychological tension and problems for the children. Terrence Gorski, an alcohol counselor who specializes in intimacy, says that almost all adult children of alcoholic families (ACOA) have problems sustaining healthy relationships.[4] Because of the way they saw their parents interact, adult children of alcoholics do not know how to recognize their own feelings and pay attention to their internal states. In alcoholic families, the drunken outbursts and conflict are looped together, either because the drinking directly leads to arguments or because an alcoholic who has been provoked will turn to liquor for comfort. As a result, both the alcoholic and the co-dependent parent try to deny or minimize differences that might lead to conflict. Believing that "all is well" in the family also works to "prove" that there really is no problem. Because feelings and differences are never allowed, an ACOA suppresses her true self and may or may not rediscover it in adulthood. If children grow up in a family where differences must be hushed, they will continue to run away from encounters with their partner when they are married. Their children, in turn, will never have the opportunity to know that it is safe to have and express a position that is different from that of others, and will not have any means of successfully resolving problems.

In alcoholic families, the focus tends to be on the "identified problem person." As a result, family members can ignore their own problems by being overly focused on someone else. While alcoholic families do have outbursts of conflict about the drinking, other issues, such as competency, lying, and trust, remain unidentified, unexpressed, and, of course, unresolved. Because the fights about the drinking are passionate, they quickly escalate into screaming battles or drinking binges, which teach children that expressed differences lead to destruction.

Unless these ways of relating are understood and changed, the pattern of the alcoholic family persists. When psychologists Carolyn and Phillip Cowan interviewed couples expecting their first child, 20 percent of the soon-to-be parents volunteered the information that they were the adult children of alcoholics. Despite the fact that there were no obvious differences between the ways these couples and other couples reacted to child rearing, the research team found that when they assessed the toddlers three years later, the children of the ACOA parents had more problems. At age five, these children were rated by their kindergarten teachers as having a more difficult time adjusting to school, and were described as being more withdrawn or more aggressive than the other children.

Clearly, the children of ACOA parents were having difficulty managing their feelings and relating to others.[5]

Overly Dependent Families

Dysfunctional families are not always alcoholic. Another family style that creates problems is "enmeshment," where pressure is put on family members to act and feel in unison.[6] In these families, there is a high degree of involvement in each other's lives, and a belief system that accentuates and rewards similarity and being alike. What is good for one is good for all. However, the harmony created in these families is costly, as individual preferences and differences are denied.

These families also operate with a high degree of anxiety about what happens when people don't agree. In most of these families, disputes that occurred among relatives in former generations have led to the total cutting off of a relationship. There are stories or memories of grandparents, aunts, and uncles who were expelled from the family, never to be spoken to again. Because these families can't tolerate differences, family members who refuse to go along with the group position are treated as ungrateful traitors. What is most important is that the current of anxiety surrounding the expression of differences is passed from one generation to the next. Because a child's noncompliance is reacted to with horror or rage, the child learns to submit to the views of the stronger person. Without the experience of being able to successfully stand up for and accept responsibility for her independent decisions, the child remains dependent on external approval and direction. As adults, children from enmeshed families continue to be fearful of difference, as it might lead to conflict and then disaster.

Living with Rose-Colored Glasses

I have worked with many couples who are not able to negotiate and work with each other's viewpoints because they can't *see* any differences between them. In some marriages, this is a shared phenomenon, as both partners tend to see things as being either all perfect or all terrible. In these marriages, which I have referred to as "roller-coaster marriages," couples tend to live in cycles. The happy phase, where all problems are denied, cannot be sustained, and sooner or later the couple plummets into the depths of despair, where differences seem overwhelming. However, there are couples with one or both partners wearing "rose-colored glasses." In this situation, one person sees things as being perfect while minor problems are minimized or completely denied. Unfortunately, if problems can't be acknowledged, they cannot be discussed and resolved. This can lead to disaster, as seen in the marriage of Howard and Penny.

HOWARD AND PENNY

Penny asked for the earliest appointment I had available, but was not sure whether she would bring her husband with her. She was convinced that her husband, Howard, was having an affair even though he denied it. The couple had recently had their third child, and Howard was a devoted father. However, since the baby had been conceived, sex had dropped off and Howard spent more time than ever at work. Still, Penny didn't think much of it until she got a phone call from the woman who claimed to be Howard's mistress. She said that she had been with him evenings, on overnight business trips, and even when Penny was in the hospital after the baby was born.

Although Howard initially denied the affair when we first met, once I explained that often an affair was an attempt to save a marriage that was failing for other reasons, he reluctantly confessed.

Penny looked at her husband in disbelief and said, "I thought you were happy. I thought we had the perfect marriage."

Howard started to speak, hesitantly, but then it was like water bursting over a dam. "You might have been happy, but I haven't been for years, and it took Tammy for me to realize it. You live for the kids and never notice whether I'm happy or not." As Penny listened through her tears, Howard continued with his list of complaints. "I hate that your sister has the keys to this house and comes and goes as she pleases. I hate how the kitchen is arranged—why can't anything turn out the way I want? You haven't really made love to me for years—not the way we used to. And the baby—well, I'm sure I'll love her like I love her sister and brother, but she was your idea, not mine!"

Penny shook her head as she answered, "I never thought you were serious. You say one thing one minute, and then you drop it. Everything else in our life is perfect. I can't believe you really think these things are so important."

In subsequent sessions, Penny explained that her mother had struggled with emphysema for fifteen years. During that time, the family had tried to stay hopeful, but they had also protected their mom and tried to make her happy in every way they knew. Penny, as the youngest daughter, was the only child at home when her mother became seriously ill. As her mother's illness progressed, Penny gave up the dates, extracurricular sports, and activities that most young women get to enjoy. One year after her mom died, Penny met Howard. She was twenty-three and had hardly dated, but she knew that he was the man of her dreams.

Penny was determined to make her new family as happy as she could. She was a most devoted mother and had a never failing reserve of energy to give to her kids. But Penny was also stubborn in her own way. As she explained, "I have a picture in my mind of how I want something to turn out, and I just keep working at it until it happens." Her dream of a close, happy family with three busy kids and people coming and going was evidently not shared by Howard, but she was oblivious to his resentment.

It was important for me to understand why Howard's concerns had not been heard. Although I could see that Penny's rose-colored glasses just let happy things in, it seemed that Howard had not tried very hard to negotiate his point of view. When I asked him about his parents' marriage, Howard shuddered and answered, "Two barracudas." It seemed that both of Howard's parents were strong individuals who fought each other for control in almost every area. Howard said that their fighting made him sick, and he had vowed never to live like that. Although Howard would pout when his decorating ideas were ignored or curse when he discovered that Penny's sister had been in the house while they were away, he hoped that Penny would pick up on his subtle protests. When she tried to minimize his concerns, he felt forced to give up. To fight would cause him to repeat his parents' marriage, something that would be more painful to him than giving in to Penny's iron will.

Howard had not wanted a third child, but once again, Penny could not hear his concerns and ambivalence. When Howard met Tammy at work, he found someone he could confide in. For the first time he felt that someone was listening and caring about his feelings, not just trying to force him into a mold. Eventually their friendship became sexual, and by the time Tammy called, she was secure in her belief that Howard would never give her up.

Speaking Through the Children

Only by voicing and standing up for what you believe in can you achieve authenticity in a relationship. Perhaps one of the most important ingredients of a truly intimate relationship is the freedom for both people to let down their guard and express their individuality.[7] When people don't vocalize their beliefs, they become distanced and lonely. Research shows that women who stop expressing themselves have higher incidents of depression, while men who stop communicating become increasingly remote and dissatisfied with their marriages.[8] At the same time, the need to communicate does not go away, which leads to detours and indirect expressions. Unfortunately, some partners who cannot directly oppose their spouses manage to get their point expressed through the children. Despite the fact that this brings the child into conflict with the other parent, this ploy is often used to influence an outcome or to get revenge. One family that stands out in my memory is the Hanzels.

THE HANZEL FAMILY

Laura Hanzel was referred to me for individual therapy because of her recurring depressions. Although Laura had been depressed a few times in high school, her episodes became more severe shortly after she got married. She also had setbacks with the birth of each of her three children, and by the time I met her, she had been hospitalized on five separate occasions for her inability to cope. In addition to times where she would be unable to get out of bed, Laura had tremendous difficulty tolerating her own anger, and would fantasize terrible acts of aggression whenever she was overstimulated or upset. She took medication to keep her fantasies in check, but would become completely quiet and withdrawn when she was confronted by anyone. It was clear to me when we first met that Laura had strong feelings about her husband, Stan. Stan, too, was deeply affected by Laura's depression, and it made sense to me that I work with them as a couple.

Stan, who was ten years older than Laura, was a very focused and controlling man. On the one hand, he had to be because Laura's emotional vulnerabilities often left her too confused and overwhelmed to run the household. But there was also a psychological component to the way this couple balanced power. Stan had been the "black sheep" in his family, the one who was considered inadequate and doomed to failure. Taking over for Laura and running their family made him feel superior and finally able to prove his family of origin wrong. However, Stan was also exhausted and frustrated. Many days he would get home from work to find Laura asleep while the laundry was piled high and there were no clean dishes with which to set the dinner table.

The eldest Hanzel daughter, Rachel, was thirteen when I first started working with the family. She often took on more than her share of responsibilities to keep the house running, but she was also able to enjoy her mother's good days and back off when Laura was able to get things done. In contrast, Stan always assumed the worst, and spoke to Laura as he would one of the children. He gave her instructions every day, with a list of chores to accomplish. Laura rarely questioned the lists or Stan's power in making most of the family decisions.

Before we started one of our sessions, I commented on a nearby restaurant that had been under construction and looked almost ready to open. I was surprised to learn that Laura had once been a good cook who enjoyed experimenting with different recipes. The pride in Laura's eyes as she told me the secrets of a good omelet was something I had never seen in her before. But now Stan had taken over planning the family's meals, and stuck to simple things in case Laura wasn't up to cooking. He even wrote out the grocery list every weekend, insisting that the food shopping be done once a week in order to make things simple.

The closest I had ever seen the couple get into a fight was when Laura muttered that it didn't make any sense to buy food a week at a time. She added, "How can you plan your menus at home when you can't even look to see what's fresh?" Stan turned red in the face and answered that he had enough to do. This was the only way he could make sure the grocery shopping got done, and it was crazy to talk about fancy cooking when the whole house was a mess. As Stan went on to complain about the clutter and filth in the living room, Laura stared vacantly at the floor.

But this was not the end of it. Although Laura never confronted Stan with her disagreement, she had ways of sabotaging his plans. As I was soon to learn, Laura would often take Rachel grocery shopping with her, and sometimes the younger children as well. Laura would say something about lunchtime or point out an expensive snack she had seen advertised on television, and before Laura knew it, one of the children would put something special in the shopping cart. Of course this would "force" Laura to improvise with Stan's menu in order to make the budget work. When Stan found out that the grocery shopping had not been carried out to his specifications, he would attack Rachel or the other children, screaming at them for wasting his hard-earned money on expensive desserts and snacks. Laura was, in his eyes, too weak to control the children, which made him even more determined to run the family the way he saw fit.

As Rachel grew older, she became more assertive with her father and less respectful of his wishes. If Stan commented on the length of her skirt, or how many nights Rachel could baby-sit that week, she would scream back to him that he was a dictator. The more rigid and controlling Stan became, the more Rachel would challenge him and do the opposite. In words and actions, Rachel told Stan what her mother felt but could not say.

Power

Once partners are able to identify areas of difference, the next step involves negotiating positions and trying to reach a resolution. The way the couple does this is largely influenced by the way power is perceived and distributed in the relationship. Power in families is an area that has received a great deal of attention from feminist scholars. The formula of women deferring to men is a subtle but persistent reality that is so ingrained in our society that it seems "normal." There is no question that children learn gender-appropriate behavior from watching their parents interact. While it is not the only explanation of how the power equation between men and women gets passed from generation to generation, many therapists believe that children model the same-sex parent when it comes to using power to settle a difference.

There are many different ways in which partners can organize power between themselves. At one end of the spectrum is a marriage where one partner is more powerful and the other partner is acquiescent or passive. If both members of the couple accept that one person has authority over the other, then the relationship can be quite harmonious and complementary. This kind of relationship is called the "traditional" marriage, and is the "norm" that most parents were exposed to when they were growing up. However, feminist scholars suggest that even when both spouses appear to be happy, there are harmful consequences to an arrangement that is perpetuated by unequal access to money, power, and safety.[9]

Today, increasing numbers of couples attempt to share power evenly so that either partner might prevail at any given moment. Typically, these couples have to work hard to accommodate each other's strengths and priorities and make sure that there is a true balance of power.[10] While many couples recognize the importance of sharing power and responsibility, most couples find this very difficult to achieve. For many years, it was believed that money was the critical factor in determining which partner had the most influence in decision making. However, in an era where women often earn equal or more money then their husbands, the formula has shifted somewhat. Recently, family therapists have suggested that perceived career importance plays an even greater role. If the husband's job is perceived as being the most important, then he will take and be given more power in the marriage. In marriages where the wife has established a respected career, she is more likely to have greater input in the decision-making process. When wives don't work, they take more responsibility for the house and the children, but have increasingly less power in other matters, such as finances and major purchases.[11]

Few couples are consciously aware of how power works in their relationship, but fall into patterns that seem almost second nature. One pattern that is quite common these days is one that family researcher John Scanzoni calls the "Junior/Senior Partner."[12] In this kind of marriage, the woman retains her sense of self by staying connected to her work or career identity, but regards her husband as the primary earner. Both partners feel respected, but develop a kind of mentor relationship in which the husband listens to and values the wife's ideas and opinions, but has greater weight in making the final decision.

I have worked with many couples who simply cannot work well together and, rather than constantly fighting, end up dividing areas where each has power and control. While designated control can never be absolute because in a shared life there is always some overlap, these partners try to avoid conflict by making one partner the "expert" in a given area. A typical arrangement might be the husband making all the decisions about major spending and saving, while the wife plans vacations and takes charge of decorating the home.

As long as both partners agree with their arrangement, they will have a relatively safe way of working things out together. The problem comes when one or both people change and no longer accept the way power has been distributed between them. Regardless of the power equation the couple originally adopted, if the marriage is based on friendship and respect, there is room for negotiation and change. In a marriage where partners feel safe and valued, their concerns can be shared openly and in good faith. Because the partners regard each other as friends, a process of communication can begin in which different perspectives can be tolerated and even validated. When partners revert to communication styles and behaviors that are not direct and respectful, there are usually underlying issues of power and control that have not been worked through.

Pathological Power

In order for a relationship to work, there needs to be a sense of mutual concern and commitment to each partner's happiness. This mutuality is often tested when there are competing needs and perspectives and each partner is determined to get his or her own way. At these moments, it is critical to understand the ways in which power can be used pathologically—that is, in ways that erode the goodwill that is an essential ingredient of healthy intimacy. There is an important distinction to be made between respectful negotiation and the abuse of power through coercion, intimidation, or domination. When a partner abuses power in order to maintain control or be the one to make a decision, the victory is a false one, for the battle that has been won cannot possibly replace what has been lost in the goodwill and affection that the marriage is built on.

Here are some of the ways in which partners can abuse power.

CALLING IN THE TROOPS

When a partner is afraid that his or her position will not prevail, one tactic used is to call on important outsiders to lend additional weight.[13] By threatening or actually involving parents, in-laws, siblings, or friends, one spouse tries to use the influence of other important relationships to accomplish what he or she could not do alone. I remember one couple whose problems started when the husband, Dan, was offered a job promotion that required the family to move across the country. His wife, Jill, who was quite content with her life, argued strongly against it, but was unable to convince Dan that the move was not in the family's best interest. Her demand for immediate marital therapy was an attempt to use another kind of power—the expert opinion. I, as the marriage therapist, was expected to side with Jill completely, and with my expert authority tell Dan that he should turn down the promotion. When I failed to deliver this message, Jill reverted to her previous power play and promptly called all of the extended family. "You're going to kill your mother," Jill declared. "She lives for her grandchildren, and you're going to take them away from her for selfish reasons!" Dan backed down, but not without considerable resentment. The children were aware that they had been used as pawns and could not respect the way either parent had handled the situation.

EMOTIONAL EXPLOSIONS

Another form of pathological power has been called "affective power," which happens when one partner becomes hysterical or emotionally distraught as a way of trying to get his or her way. In many ways, this resembles a child's temper tantrum. A child who watches an emotionally out-of-control parent may relate to his or her anguish with sympathy, but will also have no respect for that parent. The child is left with no effective role model for solving his own problems and a strong dysfunctional pattern to model. If he chooses to disidentify with the tantrum thrower, he can become emotionally collected and vow never to fall apart in such a juvenile way. In order to accomplish this, he will tend to repress or completely deny painful feelings. Another solution is for him to identify with the emotionally volatile parent and act out feelings rather than learn to contain and process intense reactions. The child is also left with complicated feelings for the parent who has backed down in the face of immature hysteria. By not standing up for his or her rights, this parent also seems weak to the child. Differences, then, become no-win situations, and emotions something to be suppressed.

PLAYING THE UPPER HAND

Sometimes differences can be resolved by one partner using resources that may be a strength in a different situation but should never be used against a partner. In some couples, this might be verbal power. Words can be used as a source of ammunition—especially when one partner is better educated or informed, and can argue his or her partner into a corner. While physical violence will be discussed in depth in Chapter Seven, the threat of abuse can be considered a form of pathological power. Once a person is exposed to violence, she will anticipate and read aggression into questionable or benign acts. The abusing partner is often able to use subtle cues to assert his power and dominate.[14] Needless to say, the threat of violence may, for the moment, squelch a partner's opposition, but it rarely leads to a harmonious or healthy resolution. Children who are exposed to negotiation that is based on intimidation and coerced acquiescence have a very dysfunctional example to model. They are left with the belief that there are only two positions in life: one of victory, gained through ruthless domination, and one of acquiescence tinged with fear. Neither will prepare a child to establish successful relationships with others or build an identity that will provide self-esteem.

WITHHOLDING RESOURCES

Any resource that one partner possesses can be used or can be withdrawn in the negotiation of differences. In marriage, this includes money, sex, and even household chores. I have known wives who, when they are upset, refuse to do their husband's laundry, and husbands who "simply don't have time" to finish a home repair project that was started in a happier moment. Walking out is a similar dynamic, for when one partner refuses to talk any further this partner is wielding power and control. Children who watch their parents interact in this way have no opportunity to watch a successful negotiation, but instead see two adults acting like children.

Negotiating Power

In all of these situations, partners have resorted to different ploys to gain power and influence, but have not developed the skills that are needed to present their arguments clearly and negotiate effectively. I have found that one reason so many couples have difficulty with negotiation is a result of power imbalances that are remnants from their family of origin. Often, partners have never developed the ability to stay with their own feelings long enough to fully comprehend their own position, and they act out their unhappiness in indirect ways. Other couples that I have worked with face potential conflict with assumptions and expectations that immediately throw them into a position where pathological power prevails. Although there are real factors to be considered in couples where there is emotional or physical abuse, too often the power imbalance is one that is perceived rather than based on actual events.

When individuals take a position because it is what they believe is expected of them or because they anticipate a chain of events, they are often being governed by beliefs that have more to do with the past than the present. This is especially true when what is influencing them is the blueprint of their own parents' marriage. When partners handle differences in the way they saw their moms and dads interact, they are most probably reverting to a power equation that does not capture what they truly want for themselves.

Children need to learn that parents can be flexible and responsive to each other. Rather than acting out power plays, parents need to learn how to talk about the ways in which different decisions are reached. By negotiating the basic rules of family life, parents can save themselves and their children from the disruption and bad feelings that are always generated by pathological power.

Talking Face-to-Face

In successful marriages, partners are able to listen and respond to each other's positions. Because the marriage is based on friendship, each partner's well-being is automatically respected. Partners in marriages where power and control are not central issues are able to value each other's opinions, as very often each can provide new information that can lead to a better joint solution. Family therapists who work with intercultural couples suggest that one way for couples to avoid problems is to create their own culture built on contributions from both partners.[15] In a way, every marriage is intercultural, for there are always differences between the partners' preferences and approaches. When couples are able to hear each other's opinion without feeling threatened or diminished, they are usually able to better understand their partner and work with rather than against their best friend.

Children who come from these families are indeed lucky. There is an atmosphere of acceptance that permits the children's viewpoints as well as the adults' to emerge. Children who watch both parents competently voice their opinions realize that both men and women have something important to contribute. Research studies show that when parents are able to disagree without becoming angry, the children are rarely affected in adverse ways. In fact, children from these homes do better in school and have higher self-esteem than do children whose parents' negotiations of differences escalate into bickering and hostile fights.[16] Children who watch their parents communicate effectively and respectfully are able to more successfully negotiate with peers and have an important head start in knowing how to resolve differences productively in the intimate relationships they will develop when they grow older.

Being able to communicate clearly and directly adds to a couple's ability to parent successfully. Children are rarely the targets of misplaced anger or are brought into conflict that does not really concern them. Instead of feeling tired and alone, parents who are able to work out their differences comfortably are able to give each other comfort and support. The joy of having a partner to share feelings with and lean on can only be sustained by resolving the challenging task of working out differences. Partners who have found ways in which to express their opinions and listen to each other are the most happily married, and this is clearly communicated to their children.

QUESTIONS

1. Who made most of the decisions in your parents' marriage? Whose opinions were most respected?

2. Whose opinion matters the most in your marriage? Do you make your decisions together, or do you split up different areas of responsibility? Do you think your style of decision making is working effectively?

3. Would the children say that one of you is really the "boss"?

4. How tuned in are you to your feelings of being frustrated or unhappy? What are your partner's cues that tell you he or she is upset?

5. Who is the one who tries to start a discussion when there are problems or differences? Do you have an established time or place to have these kinds of talks? Do the children overhear or participate in them?

6. Do you ever resent or feel frustrated with decisions that have already been made? How do you handle this?

7. Do your children ever remind you of yourself or your spouse in the way they try to establish power in their own relationships?

7
Understanding the Long-Term Effects of Conflict

"I'll Never Forget the Looks on Their Faces When We Fought"

WHEN PARTNERS CANNOT DISCUSS and resolve their differences in a fair, respectful way, or are embroiled in power struggles, then everyone is adversely affected. Every couple has issues they feel passionately different about and times when there is no compromise in sight. And while this is true for all couples, it is especially true for parents. The truth is, most couples find that having children brings them happiness but makes their marriage more stressful. Many studies have shown that couples are most likely to disagree with each other and feel unhappy about their marriage when there are children and adolescents at home. Marital satisfaction looks like the letter *U*, with high levels of happiness before children are born and when the "empty nest" is reached, but with low levels during the challenges of parenthood.

In the first year and a half after the baby is born, both husbands and wives must grapple with changes in the division of new responsibilities as well as changes in their love life.[1] When money is scarce, arguments in this area surface as well, and the couple is more likely to feel dissatisfied about their lives in general.

As seen in Chapter Six, there are many ways of dealing with differences, but too often an acceptable resolution cannot be reached and a state of full conflict emerges. Although conflict is not necessarily destructive, many couples fight in ways that lead to an erosion of goodwill and affection. Of equal importance is the fact that destructive conflict is damaging to the children. This is one area of family therapy that has been investigated in depth, and the results of the research are perfectly clear: Children who are exposed to destructive conflict are harmed. In considering marital conflict, it is possible to look at the level, frequency, and ways in which partners express their hostility as well as the related tension and withdrawal that often accompany unresolved conflict. Each has an immediately harmful effect on the child and also creates emotional scars that have long-term consequences.

When there is physical violence between the parents, the damage to the children is most severe. While most couples don't think of themselves as living in an abusive relationship, marital violence is more prevalent than people want to acknowledge. Physical aggression includes throwing household objects or slapping, things that more people do when they are angry than they would like to admit. In one research study, a large number of third- and eighth-graders were asked questions about videotapes of parents yelling at each other. Seventy percent thought that the fight might turn "physical."[2] Researchers who investigate spouse abuse think that the incidence may be as high as 40 percent, although most couples are ashamed and try to keep it private.[3]

When partners are abusive, they rarely try to protect the children from knowing about, witnessing, or even becoming involved in the violence. Judith Wallerstein, who interviewed children whose parents had been divorced, found that the majority of the children had witnessed parental abuse around the time of the separation. Most of these children were deeply upset by the violence and were unable to get over the experience. While it is not clear if the parents were abusive at other times as well, Wallerstein suggests that it is not uncommon for couples to act out their violence in front of the children. Perhaps parents want someone to bear witness to the amount of pain they are suffering; perhaps they need the security of knowing that someone is around who could step in and restrain them if things got completely out of hand. Watching a parent being punched or kicked by the other is a lesson a child will never forget.[4]

Children who are exposed to parental violence are never again quite the same. The effects can be seen in their inability to concentrate on schoolwork, and also in their peer relationships, which become strained. Girls tend to become depressed, withdrawn, and insecure, while boys become more aggressive—within the family and also toward friends and classmates. Some children who witness maternal abuse become overly attentive to their mothers, reversing the parent-child relationship and growing up well before their time.[5]

Physical aggression between parents continues to affect the child long after he has left home. As adults, these children tend to form intimate relationships that are also abusive. In fact, the best predictor of partner violence in a man is if he came from a family where he witnessed interparental violence. Women who witnessed interparental violence are especially prone to becoming victims in abusive relationships. Researchers who have followed the same families over a twelve-year time span report that parental violence increases the odds that the grown children will experience relationship violence by almost 200 percent![6]

What about when there is marital conflict but no physical violence? It used to be thought that the only harm done to children by their parents' conflict was indirect, that parents who are preoccupied by marital stress are not able to concentrate on or enjoy parenting. This is true. Research shows that mothers who are having marital problems are less playful and involved with their babies. However, as the children get older, unhappily married mothers do the opposite: They become overly involved in their children's lives in ways the children find intrusive.[7]

If marital problems lead to depression, then the children are very much affected. The majority of women who seek professional help for depression say that their relationship is their number one problem. Once depressed, a mother will become despondent and withdrawn. In such a state, she is unable to find the energy to adequately care for her children and may become passive and indifferent. Not only is there a lack of affection and fun, there is also less energy to enforce the rules.[8]

Parents in conflict definitely carry their problems into their parenting. Research studies show that these parents are more critical of their children and are more likely to discipline in inconsistent ways. For some reason, unhappy fathers are more negative toward their daughters, perhaps because they remind them of their wives.[9] Fathers in unhappy relationships tend to withdraw from the family; in addition to abdicating their role as husband, they become increasingly less involved with their kids. Tension and anger between the parents seem to spill over into the relationship one or both parents have with the children.[10] The problem is exacerbated by the reactions of the children, who tend to become more disruptive in response to the tension at home.

In addition to the consequences created by parental preoccupation, children are also negatively affected by marital tension and conflict. Over the past ten years, several important studies have clearly spelled out the harm that is done to children of all ages when they are exposed to their parents' destructive arguments. Adolescent and young adult children from families who don't know how to disagree in a constructive way have problems with anxiety, nervousness, and substance abuse.[11] While some children have immediate reactions, I have also found that for others the problems created by their parents' arguments only fully emerge when they are grown and ready to have children of their own.

When children watch adults interact in a hostile way, they immediately become anxious and distressed. This is especially so for young children, who may not understand what the ruckus is all about but are reactive to the emotional tension and discord. The more toddlers are exposed to watching their parents fight, the more insecure and disturbed they become. By covering their ears or trying to leave the room, and by becoming agitated and unable to concentrate, toddlers show their parents what they cannot tell them in words.[12]

A child who has watched his parents engage in harsh verbal conflict anticipates that this kind of argument could happen again and becomes watchful and attentive when there is any level of disagreement. Instead of staying absorbed in play, these children start paying too much attention to their parents' interactions.[13] An example of this is a darling little boy I was asked to work with several years ago.

Jordan

Jordan was brought for a full neurological workup when he was twenty months old. His parents, Ann and Steve, felt that he was hyperactive, but the doctors disagreed. Initially Ann and Steve said that everything was going fine at home and that there was not a lot of stress. However, when I asked them routine assessment questions about their health, a very different picture emerged. Steve had been diagnosed with an invasive cancer when Ann was pregnant with Jordan. He never thought he would get to see the birth of his only child, but miraculously, the cancer went into remission. Now Ann wanted a second child, and Steve was totally against it. He worried every night that the cancer would reappear and that Ann would be left a widow. This was obviously a "hot" subject, and within seconds their voices had become loud and passionate. As Ann and Steve continued their conversation, Jordan, who had been quietly playing with blocks on my office floor, started to throw his playthings and lunged for my telephone. His "hyperactive" behavior was clearly a reaction to the stress in his parents' relationship. Ann and Steve stopped their discussion, pointed to Jordan, and said to me, "See, this is exactly what he does at home." When, following my instruction, Ann and Steve were able to hold hands while they calmly talked about their different perspectives, Jordan quickly settled down to play.

Cold Wars

Small children are highly reactive to the level of tension between their parents, and are as responsive to "cold" wars as they are to screaming matches. A common pattern for couples who are fighting is to ignore their partner. As most people know, this does not take place in an emotional vacuum, but is accompanied by hostile glances and other behavior that reveals the smoldering anger. Research has shown that some children are more sensitive to this style of conflict than they are to open fights between their parents. Once again, the youngest children are the ones who react the most strongly, becoming distressed, and, over time, depressed.[14]

But older children do not do much better. Several studies have shown that preadolescent children whose fathers are in unhappy, high-conflict relationships are more dependent than are children from stable homes. Children whose mothers are unhappily married have problems with insecurity. Even women in college who report recent conflict between their parents have been found to be more susceptible to depression and relationship problems.[15] Jon Gottman, who has studied in depth the effect of parental conflict on children, has found that parents who express their hostility through contempt and belligerence usually have children who become increasingly aggressive. But the children of parents who fight by disengaging tend to internalize their problems and become depressed and anxious.[16]

The Consequences of Divorce

Current research suggests that even though divorce may be a painful experience for the children, kids who grow up in families that have chronic destructive conflict are being harmed on a more serious and more permanent basis. Several recent studies have found that children whose parents divorce respectfully and without putting the kids in the middle made excellent psychological adjustments. In contrast, kids whose parents fought viciously during or after the divorce had serious adjustment problems.[17]

Children who have lived through difficult divorces have been able to tell therapists what the worst things were for them. High on the list is being put in the middle. When one parent appeals to a child to take his or her side against the other parent, the child is put in a highly stressful, no-win situation. Having to choose sides turns both homes into war zones, and magnifies the tension that the children are already experiencing.[18] When girls are forced to see their fathers as evil, they form a negative belief about men and about the safety of marriage. A girl who is asked to take sides against her mother is left with unbearable guilt and confusion about her own ability to become a competent woman. Boys as well resent having to take sides. If a boy is asked to side with his father against his mother, he risks abandoning his primary source of nurturance and is also made to feel guilty. If he sides with his mother, he loses the opportunity to bond with his father.

When Parents Fight About the Children

Children are also extremely sensitive to the content of their parents' arguments, and become distressed when they believe they are the reason that their parents are fighting.[19] The truth is, parents frequently *do* disagree with each other about child rearing. Most parents with whom I have worked seem to believe that how their child turns out is a reflection of how good they have been at parenting. Because even minor decisions can have major consequences, most parents are ready to vigorously challenge their partner when they disagree about their partner's approach. Sadly, the energy that creates the arguments comes from the parents' love for their children, and they simply do not realize that the consequent marital tension and conflict is probably more harmful for the children than the issue that has generated the argument.

It is the rare family in which there are no differences about how the children should be raised. Most parents go back and forth about discipline, creating a seesaw where one parent's "hard" position balances the other's "soft," indulgent stance. Many men feel that their wives "baby" the children and are more tolerant and less demanding than they want them to be. The differences between men and women can be seen as early as the baby's first months. Mothers usually coo and rock their little ones while fathers offer tickles and physical stimulation.

Beyond the ways in which parents balance nurturance and stimulation there are almost always differences in the expectations that each parent has for a child. As family therapists know all too well, some of the issues that parents argue about are emotional bombs left over from problematic areas of their own childhoods. Very often a parent attempts to undo or redo his own childhood, and confuses his own feelings and experiences with his child's. Because these interactions are emotionally intense and poorly understood, a partner who attempts to intervene finds him- or herself embroiled in intense conflict.

Parents of little boys are likely to have fights about their son's masculine/feminine tendencies. Men, in particular, are often anxious and reactive to behaviors that they think are effeminate. They want their sons to develop into aggressive, self-sufficient men, and believe that the mother stands in the way of this process. For example, if a young boy becomes anxious about facing a difficult situation, or cries because he feels overwhelmed or hurt, his mother might open her arms to offer a hug or verbal reassurance. Now the father has two issues to respond to: his concern that his son is not learning how to overcome his fears in order to perform, and his worry that his boy has developed an excessive attachment to his mother. In a society such as ours where there is an unspoken fear that a weak boy will become a homosexual, and that a woman's influence leads to a life of submission, some men will undoubtedly overreact. As a result, when young boys are not being aggressive or active enough, their fathers respond by teasing them, ridiculing them, or even calling them names such as "sissy." In an effort to protect his son, the husband may also accuse his wife of causing their son's unacceptable feminine behavior, and attack her in ways that lead to a fight. Unfortunately, most of these arguments happen spontaneously, and in front of the child. Rather than correct the situation, this kind of behavior usually leads to profound feelings of inadequacy and resentment, both in the mother as well as the son.

As the mother of an eight-year-old boy, I find that it is not uncommon to see this kind of interaction in public places such as the community skating rink or soccer field. It is painful for me to watch my friends and neighbors fly into these kinds of arguments when their sons take a spill and start to cry. If the boy doesn't pick himself up and completely disregard his pain or fear, his father will become irate and intolerant. Should the mother step in to offer a hug or try to soothe away the boy's tears, too many fathers will become hostile and blame the mother for ruining their son. Mothers who accept this verdict and turn away leave their sons feeling both abandoned and responsible for causing his parents great unhappiness. While the trait of male self-reliance has been reinforced, it has prevailed at the expense of other emotional needs—a formula that many psychologists believe leads to alienation and emotional disconnection.[20]

Fighting Through the Children

Fights about the children often have nothing to do with the children. Very often parents are fighting about things that involve themselves but that they have not had the courage or awareness to discuss before. In some situations, a parent might believe that he or she is not really bothered or affected by some issue, or that it is not worth the potential conflict to bring it up. However, the same behavior in a child might stimulate the parent to attack with blazing guns. Similarly, what could be denied as being important for oneself is fiercely overreacted to when it concerns the child. The Stanton family exhibited this pattern of behavior.

THE STANTON FAMILY

John and Meridith Stanton started couples therapy on the advice of Meridith's individual therapist. Meridith had started treatment for depression, which her therapist thought was related to marital problems. The couple had been married for twenty years and had two teenage daughters. On the surface, they were a happy family, but many problems had been denied or swept aside in order to maintain this facade.

John was a charismatic, intelligent man who deeply loved his wife and daughters. John came from a poor family, and as the middle of five children did not receive a great deal of attention. When I asked him about his parents' marriage, John answered that his parents had a pretty good marriage, but that money was something they fought about all the time. John felt that his father, especially, was a failure who could never bring home enough money to keep his family fed. As a result of the financial pressures, John dropped out of school just before graduation and started a business, which over the years had prospered and grown. Meridith had also felt neglected throughout childhood, as her mother had to shoulder the responsibilities of caring for an ill sister and a chronically ill child at the same time. In order to keep the situation under control, her mother had become "an autocrat" who bossed everyone around and had no time for "small talk." Beyond that, Meridith's parents spent little time together and seemed preoccupied with other interests and commitments. Meridith had learned to keep her feelings to herself, and spent hours alone in her bedroom playing the guitar.

The early years of the marriage had gone relatively smoothly, as Meridith had conceived immediately and both she and her husband truly enjoyed being parents. In most ways, John was the leader of the family, making decisions about which house to live in, which cars to buy, and how to spend vacations. While Meridith was slow to understand her feelings or get inspired, John was full of creative energy and plans. However, most of John's ideas worked out well, and Meridith grew less and less confident about expressing opinions that might interrupt the way things were going. Eventually, Meridith began to feel totally taken over by John. He gave advice on how to handle a variety of situations, from dealing with the girls' teachers to handling a dispute with the dry cleaner. Over the years, Meridith had grown more detached and depressed, so that she rarely looked forward to spending time with her husband and seldom approached him to talk.

The spring that I started working with the couple was an interesting one. Their elder daughter, Kim, was in her freshman year of college and totally undecided about what subject to major in. She was also planning to come home for the summer, and had mentioned to her dad that she needed to find a job. I had been slowly exploring Meridith's awareness and feelings about her powerlessness within the marriage and the anger stuffed inside her. I had also started probing for John's feelings of resentment at having a wife who seemed so inadequate and dependent. However, things were relatively calm until Kim's visit home.

John had given Kim a list of business associates he thought might hire her for the summer, and had started to talk to her about the advantages of focusing on a major early in her education. When Meridith overheard this discussion, she exploded. Meridith started to scream that it was time for John to let Kim lead her own life. She didn't need to be pressured by him and do everything his way. She was capable of making her own decisions and shaping her own life. John snarled back that it was time Kim learned what life was really like, and the importance of becoming accountable.

At my urging, the couple continued their fight in our session. This time, I asked Meridith to say "we" instead of "Kim," and John to say "both of you." Within minutes, the couple realized that they were not fighting about Kim at all. For the first time they were facing their own differences head on. While it took the couple months to be able to fully express and understand their resentments and wish for change, they were both able to go home after that session and apologize to Kim for having drawn her into a fight that was truly not about her.

Children as Peacemakers

Children also resent having to become the "peacemakers" in the family. When parents squabble, children do their best to stop the conflict. Just the other day, my five-year-old interrupted a heated discussion between my husband and myself. "Mummy, you go into the dining room, and Daddy you go into the kitchen for five minutes until you can learn to talk nice to each other." Her "time-out" was not too different from the way I handle fights between her and her brother, but the strength with which she interrupted the conflict showed me how upset she was.

In families where the parents' arguments have led to physical aggression, the children are even more apt to try to intervene. Fearing that things might get out of control again, kids take action that will break up the fight before it gets too destructive. However, trying to break up the fight is something that kids resent having to do, especially because they might suddenly become the targets of their parents' anger.[21] Many children feel they have been scapegoated or picked on by parents who were taking out their anger unfairly. Perhaps they are right. Even when they can shield themselves from one parent's anger, being the peacemaker puts an unfair burden on a child. One young woman who was deeply affected by this kind of situation was Helen.

HELEN

Helen was referred after a suicide attempt when she was seventeen years old. Although she had a beautiful face, Helen was at least sixty pounds overweight, and for years had been teased by other children. The crisis that led Helen to want to kill herself was getting a scholarship to a prestigious university. While her immigrant parents thought Helen should go to a local college or perhaps work full-time and put herself through school at night, Helen had wanted something different for herself. She was extremely bright, and worked hard to achieve good grades. With high SAT scores and the encouragement of her guidance counselor, she had applied for and won a wonderful scholarship.

However, Helen was conflicted about leaving the family. For

years, her parents had fought bitterly and seemed to hate each other. Helen's mother routinely talked to her daughter about how miserable she was. Every day after school Helen's mother would give her daughter milk and cookies while she complained about how her father had demanded sex the night before or had refused to give her enough money for groceries. While her mother ranted on, Helen would eat . . . and eat and eat. When her parents were fighting, Helen's mother would use Helen as a go-between. "Tell your father that it's time for his dinner. . . . Tell your father to stop being so angry at me. . . . See if your father will give you some extra money so I can get a new sweater for you. . . ."

Now Helen had a chance to make all of her dreams come true, but she felt that if she left home, her mother would not be able to cope. Unable to turn to a needy mother or a father she had learned to despise, her only solution was to kill herself.

Children as Detours

Children who are exposed to parental conflict may find another strategy to solve the family tension and discord. Too many youngsters discover that by becoming the "problem" they force their parents to drop whatever they were fighting about in order to work together on their shared concern. This pattern was identified thirty years ago and has been confirmed in recent research studies on children who have a broad range of behavioral and psychosomatic problems.[22]

Parents are not usually aware that they have deflected attention away from their own differences in order to respond to the "special needs" of a child. In research studies, these kinds of couples report little marital conflict, and instead describe their child's problems in depth. However, couples who have a solid marriage and a healthy family profile are different, because they more readily acknowledge and identify differences rather than completely deny them. In families where parents deny the existence of marital problems, the children are usually aware of the differences. They talk about their parents' problems in getting along and blame themselves for causing the tensions. Many develop additional symptoms that indicate underlying depression and anxiety.[23]

PARENTIFIED CHILDREN

When a child like Helen is drawn into her parents' conflict either as a peacemaker, a go-between, or a target, she ceases being a child with few responsibilities and instead takes over the burdens of her parents. Now the child takes over the caretaking, while her parents continue in their irresponsible, childish ways. Gregory Jurkovic describes how this leads to the creation of a "parentified" child who is harmed in ways few parents would ever intend.[24] The children who get put into this position tend to come from families where there is dysfunctional conflict and/or divorce, substance abuse, or economic situations that leave a parent overwhelmed and incapable of handling his or her responsibilities. By being forced to grow up before her time, the child develops a pervasive mistrust of adults. In addition, parentified children often develop low self-esteem and continue their dutiful pattern of putting other people's needs first. It is not uncommon for them to find themselves perpetually taking care of others, and even seeking intimate relationships that will ensure this pattern.

Other Problems That Surface in Adulthood

The consequences of growing up with destructive or chronic conflict are often not fully appreciated until much later in the child's life. Judith Wallerstein, who learned a great deal about the long-term consequences of parental conflict in her follow-up studies of children of divorce, calls this the "sleeper" effect.[25] Even though some children appeared to be making an excellent adjustment five years after their parents' divorce, they often developed serious problems when they left home and began to face the prospect of developing their own intimate relationships. At this point, the memories of their parents' bitterness were reawakened, leading to mistrust, doubts, and self-destructive behavior.

Another way that children are affected by their parents' conflict is by heightened sensitivity to interpersonal tension and conflict. Research studies have shown that children who see their parents act in aggressive ways start to interpret neutral actions as being hostile. In other words, they come to expect conflict, and see it in situations that are not at all conflictual. Unfortunately, this style of perception is not limited to the days of immediate exposure, but rather becomes a lifelong scar, as the underlying mechanisms of perception and attribution have been altered.[26]

In my marital therapy practice, I am constantly helping couples check their reactions to each other's statements and actions. When a person interprets his partner's comments as being sarcastic or demeaning, he will respond in a defensive or attacking way. However, many times the original comment was taken out of context or was completely misunderstood. Instead of asking his partner to clarify what she meant, too often the spouse will assume that his appraisal of the situation is accurate. In my experience, the couples who have the worst problems with this grew up in homes where there was frequent and destructive marital conflict. These people have come to expect that undermining and hostility are the predominant qualities of marriage, and experience it even when it is not happening. A perfect example of this is found in Peter and Catherine.

PETER AND CATHERINE

Peter and Catherine are the couple I told you about in the introduction who called after hearing me speak at a workshop. I was touched when they asked me to help them with their marriage—"for their baby's sake"—and found them to be open and motivated to work on their marriage. Some of the things they fought about were related to financial pressures, as Catherine had taken four months off from work after the baby came and was hoping to keep a half-time work schedule until Amy was comfortably settled in a prekindergarten or nursery. Peter was self-employed, and for unknown reasons his business had recently dropped off dramatically. Although Peter had worked hard to set himself up in business and loved his work, he was seriously considering taking a job with an established company just to have a steady income. Because Catherine's family had been fairly affluent, she expected to be able to do things for Amy and was frustrated that she could not give her daughter the life she wanted for her. Whenever she saw another mother buying clothes for her daughter that she knew would be perfect for Amy, she would be overwhelmed by envy. If she broke down and bought the outfit, Peter would hit the roof. But if she passed it by, she would think about it all night and explode at Peter for some small thing he did or didn't do.

Many couples fight about money and spending, but not with the intensity of this couple. They knew that it was a loaded issue, but could not figure out how to approach each other more constructively. I suggested that it would be helpful to learn about their childhood situations, and asked them to tell me more. Peter said that he didn't have a very good relationship with either one of his parents. He said that his mother was the "Queen of Criticism," but that his father was even worse. "Nothing that I did was ever good enough. . . . He acted like he was entitled to everything." When I asked Peter if this was also true for his parents' marriage, he quickly added, "My dad was even more demanding of my mom than of me. I think that it was contagious, from him to her and then to all three kids."

I asked Peter if he thought there were any similarities between his life now and then. At first he didn't see any, but then he started to connect the feeling he experienced when Catherine couldn't get "enough" spending money, and how his father used to make him feel. "I think that Catherine is completely ungrateful. I don't even think that she realizes how much I am giving her by taking on all the financial pressure while she works less than half-time." Catherine jumped in to protest that that simply wasn't true. "I try to say things to Peter all the time, but he simply doesn't hear. And I do feel bad when I can't get the baby special things. But that probably comes from my family's issues."

Catherine went on to explain that her father was an architect who made quite a bit of money, but who was very stingy. "It's funny. We had a boat, and went on family vacations, but my mother was always fighting to be able to buy clothes or furniture. My dad is still that way now. They never go to fancy restaurants even though they can afford to and my mom would love to. I guess when you come down to it, they spend money on what my father wants." I asked Catherine to tell me more about her parents' marriage. "Well, in some ways it was a lot like my in-laws'. My mom wasn't as critical, but my dad was really mean to her quite a bit. He had very high expectations for everyone, and he would go wild if things were not handled in the way he wanted."

I commented that two themes seemed to overlap for both of them. One was the idea of being dominated by an insatiable, ungrateful partner and the other was a view of a partner as demanding perfection and rejecting anything less. Together, Catherine and Peter started to figure out how these themes crept into their marriage. Peter was the first to recognize that he often thought Catherine was seeing him as inadequate and that her needs were never ending. "She doesn't have to come out and say it. It's just the way she looks at me. And then I get furious at her. I think, You ungrateful bitch! You have to get everything you want or I'm worthless to you." Catherine said, "I think that sometimes I do expect to get everything I want. I don't always know how Peter's business is going, and sometimes I think that Peter is withholding from me. He's doing things his way and putting me last. But he's so sensitive to criticism. If I say one thing that I wish could be different, he just stops listening. Why should I have to pretend that everything's perfect if it's not?"

It did not take long for Catherine and Peter to see how these ways of interpreting events were turning their life into a replay of their parents' marriage. Catherine anticipated that Peter was going to be withholding and was resentful when she thought this was happening. Peter frequently assumed that Catherine was critical and dissatisfied with him as a provider and as a partner. Her silence was often taken as a sign of disapproval. Once I saw how the couple's beliefs and expectations led them to distort what was really happening, I started interrupting each to ask, "What do you think your partner is thinking right now?" When Peter and Catherine took the time to check out their assumptions to see if they were accurate, the majority of the time they discovered that they had read something into their partner's response that simply was not there. But once old themes and anger took over, they were incapable of seeing each other as anything but ghosts from the past. Therapy involved helping them challenge and shift their expectations so that they could verify that they were truly there to love and support each other. By validating each other and acting in loving ways, they could fight the mistrust that so quickly led to distance and bad will.

Catherine called me a few months after our last session to tell me that things were still going well. She and Peter now talked about how lucky they were to have each other and their beautiful daughter, and felt that they were really on each other's side. The tension that had once robbed them of their family closeness was a thing of the past.

Do's and Don'ts of Conflict

Very few parents want to do anything purposefully to hurt their child, yet too few parents understand how harmful certain kinds of conflict between them are to their children. At the same time, the research on family conflict cited throughout this chapter points us toward successful solutions—ways of handling conflict that are constructive for both children and parents. Here are some do's and don'ts on the ways of handling conflict.

DON'T FIGHT ABOUT THE CHILDREN IN FRONT OF THE CHILDREN

Children who observe their parents fighting about them are in particularly vulnerable positions. Because children typically see themselves at the center of events, it is not uncommon for young children to blame themselves for causing their parents' arguments. Obviously this is confirmed in the childrens' minds when the problems that are destroying their family's peace are caused by them. Saddled with this guilt, children blame themselves in ways that translate into low self-esteem or behavioral problems.

DO LIMIT THE EMOTIONAL PITCH

Conflict can be considered destructive when the anger and emotional reactions are excessive, when partners verbally abuse each other, even by name-calling or swearing, or when there are threats of violence or of ending the marriage. When conflict is destructive, it is much harder to find a good or productive resolution of the problem precipitating the argument. People who are fighting with this intensity have reached a state of "high arousal." Increased adrenaline puts them in a "fight or flight" mode, which in turn prevents them from processing new information. When spouses are in a heated exchange, they are incapable of working out their differences. Because partners have not been able to take in or respond to each other's viewpoints, nothing useful comes out of this kind of argument. All that happens is a rupture of the couple's intimacy, so that partners feel worse about each other and the problem than they did before the fight.[27] Equally important is the sad reality that when parents have reached this peak of emotional tension they are not available to their children at all.

DON'T AVOID TALKING ABOUT DIFFERENCES

Conflict, per se, is not destructive. Couples who are afraid of conflict and who choose not to talk out their differences often have more problems in their marriages than do couples who have learned how to talk about issues openly. Couples who don't talk about their problems become increasingly unsatisfied, and have less intimacy over time. Furthermore, children who do not have the chance to see conflict being handled in a constructive way do not get to learn ways of managing differences in their own lives. Only by watching productive ways of resolving conflict can children learn to model these important skills.

DO FIGHT FAIR

When a partner is able to identify a concern and present it in a way that is not blaming or vindictive, it is easier to engage in a collaboration. Constructive marital disagreements allow partners to express their feelings in an atmosphere of empathy and understanding. Rather than making attacking accusations that lead to retaliation or withdrawal, constructive disagreement occurs in an atmosphere of safety. Partners may disagree, but they listen and try to understand each other's viewpoint. Children who see their parents fight like this are learning that differences are not necessarily frightening and that disagreements do not destroy feelings of love. Experiments have shown that infants and toddlers continue to smile, laugh, and play throughout their parents' quarrels when the quality of the interaction is not emotionally hostile.[28]

The level of anger and emotional distress that children observe when their parents fight filters into their sense of well-being and security.

Rather than trying not to fight in front of their kids, parents need to learn how to fight constructively. Parents who have violent arguments when the children are sleeping are fooling themselves if they believe they are not harming their kids. Almost all of my adult clients who have problems with conflict in their marriages speak about memories of lying in their beds at night, trembling as they listened silently to their parents' shouting. It is not unhealthy for children to know that their parents disagree; it is only damaging for them to be in a home with destructive conflict.

DON'T BRING YOUR CHILDREN INTO THE MIDDLE

As illustrated by the case of Helen, it is extremely painful and damaging to a child to be asked to take sides. By making a child interact with one parent on behalf of the other, the child is forced into an oppositional relationship with that parent. While the parent may feel less alone, the child has been brought into an adult arena that is truly none of his business. Because children are eager to help restore peace to the family, they may accept a parent's request to be on their side, but not without immediate and long-term consequences. While many parents can feel secure in the knowledge that they have not purposefully sought a child's alliance, there are many occasions on which children volunteer their involvement in order to help solve the conflict. Parents who care about their children's well-being should be alert to this kind of response, and should make every effort to keep their children out of their marital problems. When it comes to conflict, triangles simply aren't worth it.

Do Reassure Your Children
When They Get Upset by a Fight

When a child is distressed by his parents' fights, he is alone with his fears and worries. While his parents might be there to comfort or soothe him at other times of distress, they are not available to him in the middle of their arguments. The young child often feels panicked, expecting something terrible to happen to one or both of his parents, and feeling helpless because he cannot stop the fight. This combined sense of anxiety and helplessness upsets a child and gets absorbed into the child's belief system, so that differences become a source of anxiety.

Children are especially reactive to their parents' threats to leave or divorce. While the parents might know that things said in anger are often not true, younger children have no way to be certain about what grown-ups are going to do next. Threats to break up the family affect their sense of security and well-being and are never taken lightly.

Remember that kids tend to blame themselves when things go wrong. Even when parents are fighting about matters that are totally unrelated to the children, kids need to hear that Mom and Dad are disagreeing about friends or money but that they are not angry at them.

Don't Confide in Your Children
About Your Marital Problems

It is amazing to me what some parents choose to confide in their children. While intimacy involves sharing, this does not mean that parents are allowed to put burdens on their children's shoulders. Children should be free to confide their worries and concerns to their parents; parents should tell children only what is necessary for them to understand about issues that affect them directly. Marital intimacy and sex are not things that children need to be informed about. When a child is exposed to private matters, he is put in a terrible position. The parent disclosing the marital problems is essentially asking the child to support him and to join with him against the other parent. The unspoken or perhaps spoken message is, "Your other parent has done terrible things to me. Because I have been made so unhappy, you must give all your love to me to help me feel better, and you must do what you can to punish the person who has hurt me so badly."

Children might fantasize about their parents' sexual relationship, but they are made anxious and uncomfortable by the facts. The truth is, learning about the details of a parent's sex life is overstimulating for the child, and causes noticeable symptoms of distress. Adolescents are equally unprepared to hear about the intimate details of their parents' marriage. At least they are more able to protect themselves, even though they may be forced to emotionally or physically leave the situation entirely.

Do Acknowledge in Front of the Child That the Fight Is Over

Unfortunately for children, most parents do make up after their arguments, but choose to do so in private. A child has no idea that his parents have made peace, apologized, and perhaps even made love. While many parents may assume that because their argument was private they don't have to report to the children that they have stopped quarreling, research suggests the opposite. When children have a chance to see their parents end a fight, they get to see for themselves that all is well again. In research experiments, children who watched their parents make up immediately relaxed and became free from their symptoms of distress.[29] While this does not mean that parents have to time their fights so that they can make up in front of the kids, it does mean that once the quarrel has been resolved, there should be some public mention of it. To the extent that parents are aware of how distressed the kids were during the quarrel, it might not be a bad idea to acknowledge that the fight was stressful for everyone, and that Mom and Dad feel bad that it ever happened.

Do Balance Anger with Love and Humor

At the end of the day, parents will always have their differences, and will always have things to fight about. Psychologists who study conflict suggest that the most important ingredient in maintaining a child's psychological health is to balance the emotional life of the family so that there is as much or more warmth and affection as there is tension and hostility. In families where there are strong marriages, parents laugh with each other and with their children. These children carry their sense of humor into other situations, and use it to successfully resolve differences when problems emerge in other relationships. When children feel that their basic family life is secure, they are more able to tolerate moments of tension and conflict.

QUESTIONS

1. How did your parents fight? Open wars? Withdrawal and distance? Physical acts like kicking or slapping? How aware were you of their fights? Did you ever find yourself in the middle?

2. Are you ever afraid of "really" losing your temper? Have you found ways to control it?

3. Are you ever afraid that your partner might "really" lose his or her temper? How does this affect your relationship?

4. How often do you and your partner fight in front of your children? Do you think it bothers them in any way?

5. How often do you make up in front of your children, or let them know that a fight is over?

8
Emphasizing the Positives

"Laughing Together and Enjoying Each Other Are Part of Who We Are"

G IVEN ALL THE THINGS that can and do go wrong in a marriage, it is important to focus on the positive things that keep a relationship alive and well. For as we have seen, when the marriage is strong, it is the children who benefit—on a daily basis, and for years to come. Psychiatrist Jon Gottman, a leading marriage researcher, suggests that in order to keep a relationship working, there needs to be a certain ratio of good to bad. The magic number is not fifty-fifty, but five to one![1] For every stressful or negative interaction, there need to be five positive ones. Described below are the positive aspects most visible to children. Each should be considered from a dual perspective: for the goodness it brings to the marriage, and for the positive lesson of love it teaches the next generation.

Physical Affection

One thing that stands out in couples who have been happily married for longer than twenty years is the extent of physical touching that goes on between partners.[2] While sex is also important to the marital relationship, being able to show affection in nonsexual ways adds to the sense of caring and closeness. My husband's touch is one of the most precious things I can count on. It is amazing how relaxed and comforted I become when he strokes my arm. There are a hundred ways to express affection physically, ranging from a good-morning hug to holding hands on a walk. Most couples don't need a list of ideas, they need to be pushed into taking a risk.

The couples I work with who are in the most trouble are physically distant even when they are not in immediate conflict. When I ask them about this, I am usually told that they don't want to be rejected, or that they don't feel like having sex and don't want to appear to be sending mixed messages. As a result, they think that by keeping physically apart they are avoiding tension and conflict. This couldn't be farther from the truth. Touching is a soothing way to bring connection to a relationship. Even partners who may be frustrated by a lack of sexual intimacy will usually be appreciative of affection.

Children may be made uncomfortable by their parents' overt displays of sexuality, but they usually enjoy and benefit from physical displays of affection. In fact, most of the time they will join in for their share of hugs! When children see evidence of physical affection between their parents, their sense of security is enhanced beyond words. By incorporating the vision of parents touching or holding hands into their schema, they are likely to expect this and search for a partner who is equally comfortable with hugs and physical closeness. When the family environment feels secure and warm, children are free to engage in the normal pursuits of childhood. Watching Mom and Dad hug or hold hands will stay in their minds for a lifetime as a signal of family peace and a dream for their own future.

Friendship

Another quality that is high on the list of happily married couples is friendship, which includes sharing interests as well as thoughts. Once again, there is no set formula for how much time spouses must spend together in shared activities for a marriage to work. But it is definitely clear that partners who have things to talk about that are interesting to both have a distinct advantage in keeping their marriage happy. When parents have only the home and children in common, it is easy for conversations to become problem-focused. Couples also need to have fun together and enjoy each other as companions, not just as co-parents.

Parents who share hobbies and interests have lively and engaging conversations for their children to overhear. Because this kind of marriage is stimulating and fun, the children are likely to incorporate the belief of marriage as friendship into their schema. Bringing fun and friendship into a marriage can provide a couple with nourishment that sustains them in the hard times and gives them even more reason to keep working to keep their marriage vital. A couple who really benefited from this was Alan and Megan.

ALAN AND MEGAN

Megan was surprised when Alan said that he was unhappy and was wondering if they would be happier apart. Jolted out of a sense of complacency, she immediately pressured Alan to start couples therapy. Alan struck me as being a very low-key, easygoing man, and I wondered what had sparked his interest in separating. He assured Megan that he had no outside romantic interests, but said that he was finding himself bored and wishing there was more to life. Megan agreed that things between them were a little boring. Each spouse was involved extensively in their careers and committed to the well-being of their two teenage daughters. However, the eldest was ready to graduate from college, and the younger one would be leaving home the following year. Often Alan found himself staring at Megan and wondering what they could talk about. Megan laughed when she heard this and answered, "That happens all the time to me, too. You know, I have girlfriends that I can talk to, but most of the time we're together, I can't think of anything to say."

Despite their obvious distance, the goodwill and trust shared by this couple permeated the room. Megan suggested that Alan's sudden interest in relating was probably due to the fact that his business had slacked off a little. "When Alan is busy, he has no time for me at all. I bet that if his business picks up in the next month, he'll brush this whole thing aside and insist that he's too busy for therapy." Alan agreed that this was probably true, but added, "I think it's also getting ready to turn fifty. I never thought I would be a candidate for a midlife crisis, but I suddenly think that I have wasted an important area of my life, and really want a relationship that has more excitement."

Rather than becoming defensive, Megan grew silent and then added, "Maybe you're right. I came today because I didn't want to end our marriage, but now I think I want what you do just as much. And even if you get busy at work again, I want us to make our marriage a priority."

As I became familiar with some of the issues that affected this couple, I could identify problems in the way they avoided conflict. They also had not resolved important issues concerning money and the children. But beyond that, there was a fundamental problem in that they seemed to have very little in common. In order to help stimulate this part of their relationship, I asked them to imagine a scene where they were having fun together.

Alan imagined riding bicycles and having a private picnic in a beautiful, remote meadow. Megan said that she hardly knew how to swim, but that she had always wanted to sail. Her fantasy was the two of them sailing peacefully on a beautiful summer day. I asked them how difficult it would be to think about each other's dream and imagine being there with their partner. Alan and Megan started to joke about getting on a bicycle for the first time after twenty years, but there was a feeling of acceptance and curiosity.

Although I do not always assign homework, I asked the couple to investigate both of their fantasies and see if it was possible to take the first step. In the meantime, the therapy focused on helping the couple talk through some painful issues in a safe environment. Alan and Megan realized that part of the reason they had run out of things to talk about was their shared need to avoid any subject that might be conflictual. Because there were so many subjects that held unresolved problems, few topics could be raised safely. Learning how to stay with and finish discussions about problems was an important turning point, but equally important was building new interests into the relationship. By the time this couple had finished marital therapy, they had purchased bicycles and started building up their endurance on weekend outings. They had received brochures from three sailing schools, and seemed intent on signing up. In addition, they had chosen to go out for breakfast together one morning each week, and giggled as they told me how much fun it was sneaking out of the house for some private time together. Now the couple had a lot to talk about. They were not afraid of revisiting hot topics, and were genuinely interested in their new "outdoor" relationship.

Although Alan and Megan had not originally spoken about their children's problems, they were mutually concerned but on opposite sides of a situation involving their elder daughter, Sharon. Never the best student, Sharon had struggled to find a field that interested her, and had switched her major three times. While Alan was more patient and understanding of his daughter's lack of direction, Megan was annoyed that Sharon had not approached her studies with much commitment, and felt that much of her education was "wasted." The thought of paying for yet another year of undergraduate studies made Megan furious, and she was angry at Alan for not taking a stand. As we spoke together about Sharon's career confusion, it became clear that Alan spent a great deal of time on the phone coaching and counseling his daughter. Alan had never received much attention or support from his own parents, and his relationship with Sharon was gratifying for both of them. However, he could see how his position made it too easy for Sharon to avoid taking responsibility for herself, and he eventually agreed to a compromise with Megan. When Sharon asked for yet another semester's tuition, her parents announced that they would pay only half of the school-related expenses. Sharon surprised them by declaring that she was ready to graduate after all, and had set up an interview for a part-time job that sounded interesting to her. It seemed that when Sharon knew her parents were ready for her to grow up, she was happy to oblige. Their newly found enjoyment and unity had surely given her the safety she needed to move ahead with her own life.

Appreciation

Happily married couples are able to add to each partner's sense of well-being by demonstrating appreciation. Women who work say that when their husbands let them know that they are appreciated, then everything seems "do-able." It is only when they feel taken for granted that the burdens of both work and running the home create resentment. Many partners are grateful that they have each other to help with the children, but few take the time to say it. In fact, most research on families shows that wives think they do more than their husbands say they do, and husbands think they do more than their wives give them credit for.[3]

Parents who express their recognition of what a good parent their partner is add to the sense of well-being in the marriage and in the family. Simple words of recognition for a job well done go a long way in making a marriage feel positive. Part of the joy of loving someone comes from the reciprocal feelings of being needed and valued. When this is present, partners feel renewed in their commitment to each other and have the energy to invest in all other areas of their lives. When parents are able to validate each other's hard work and express their appreciation, the children are the ones who really win. In this situation they get the best of both worlds: parents who are emotionally available when needed but who are not dependent on their children to fulfill unmet intimacy needs. Best of all, they have the vision of a loving relationship to identify with.

When unresolved conflict and disappointments rob partners of their warm feelings toward each other, each is left feeling uncared for and unsupported. It is not uncommon for people to get discouraged when things are not going well and to let their pessimism about one aspect of the relationship contaminate their feelings about other areas. By failing to notice and say something about the good things that their partners *are* bringing into their lives, the cycle of disappointment and negativity gets worse. Recognition of the positives can help turn this around, and can rekindle the potential for warmth and closeness.

When children are around parents who are bitter and distant, they learn that the dream of "happily ever after" love is fraudulent. The lack of appreciation displayed by their parents creates a sense of marriage as unfriendly and unrewarding. Children whose parents are able to validate and acknowledge each other's contributions see how important partners can be to each other. The goodwill and positive feelings that are generated through appreciation teach children the importance of praise, and they are more likely to be comfortable both receiving and providing it in their relationships with others.

Laughter

Being able to laugh together has also been cited as one of the key ingredients of a happy marriage.[4] Having a sense of humor can often help partners keep problems in perspective. This does not mean that all issues and differences should be joked away, but there needs to be a way to separate out those things that are serious from the things that simply must be adjusted to. When parents can laugh together and use humor to get past difficult moments, the children are also spared the tension that in other families creates angst and worry. Children are more likely to use humor in their own friendships and to carry on the family tradition when they marry.

There is a story in my family that gets told over and over again. My grandmother, who was an excellent cook, had worked all day to make a huge pot of chicken soup and matzo balls to bring to her daughter's house for the family seder. My grandfather carried the prized soup carefully, but somehow slipped on the front porch. As the story goes, my grandmother watched, horrified, as her hours of hard work dribbled down the front steps, then burst out laughing. My grandparents were still laughing when they arrived at the seder, and could hardly explain why there would be no soup that night without bursting into giggles again. These wonderful people knew that there were more important things in life than the soup, and that to ruin their day or the family seder would not bring back the matzo balls. My grandmother never thought for one second that my grandfather had sabotaged her hard work on purpose—he was the greatest fan of her cooking! Their sense of humor and love for each other spared them from what, for a different kind of couple, would have been a ruined evening.

Open-Mindedness

The longer I practice therapy, the more respect I have for the importance of beliefs. So many behaviors and events can be interpreted to mean something different from what was intended. Research on communication confirms the importance of attributes, or the meaning that a person "reads in" to make sense of a situation. In one research experiment, husbands, wives, and outside raters were shown videotapes of the couple talking to each other. Each person was asked to evaluate and score specific sentences as being positive, neutral, or negative. What the researchers discovered was that spouses in happy marriages rated their partners' comments as being predominantly neutral or positive, and assumed goodwill and good intentions. However, in the unhappy relationships, partners perceived each other's comments and actions to be unkind and negative. Even when the rater scored a comment as being neutral, the conflictual spouses believed that their partner's statement was negative. Neutral comments were heard as being negative, and positive statements were evaluated as being neutral.[5] A negative bias leads to greater discord, while positive evaluations add to marital harmony and satisfaction.

It is not accurate to conclude that people should automatically focus on the positive, for there is always the risk of glossing over something "negative" that is important to hear and respond to. But people should consider the possibility of alternative intentions, and become more open-minded to different ways of seeing and understanding things. Parents who look for the positive in each other's actions are more tolerant and more likely to forgive. By believing in each other's good intentions, they guard their relationship from the jaded perceptions and distortions that take over when pessimism prevails.

So often, people are hurt, angered, or disappointed by something they have incorrectly concluded. Unfortunately, rather than stop to talk about the incident, they take a reactive or defensive posture, which invariably puts into motion the very interaction that was misconstrued. In therapy, I often have to help couples slow down their communication by asking them, "What did that mean to you?" and then have them check back with their partner to see if they had lost or distorted the intended meaning. Learning to question their assumptions made a big difference for Gail and Mario.

Gail and Mario

In our very first session, I told Gail and Mario that they were the most reactive couple I had ever worked with. They were completely tuned in to each other's tone of voice and body language, so that the slightest gesture became evidence of an unexpressed belief. Unfortunately, the messages they looked for and therefore "discovered" were statements of rejection and criticism. In the beginning of therapy, it was extremely challenging for me to make sense of their interaction. Gail started to explain her side of a story, and then stopped mid-sentence to hurl an accusation at Mario. "Don't deny that . . . you know this is exactly what happened." Puzzled, I asked Gail why she had said that. "I can tell what he is thinking," she insisted. "He never takes responsibility for his actions." When I finally got Gail to back up in explaining how she had realized that Mario was denying her side of the story, she told me firmly that she knew by the way Mario looked at the wall. I have worked with couples long enough to know that sometimes they do know each other very well, but Mario's gaze had not conveyed anything to me and he had appeared to be listening to his wife. When I asked Mario if he had felt resentful or upset about his wife's version of the story, he admitted that he was starting to get upset but insisted that he was doing his best to listen. "She always tells me what I am thinking or what I am feeling, but she's usually wrong," Mario protested.

Moments later, the reverse interaction occurred. While Mario was telling his version of the story, Gail tensed her neck as if to relax tension. Mario stopped speaking to stare accusingly at her, and then said to me in a tone of utter pessimism, "What's the use? She'll never change; there's no point in talking about it." I am usually very attentive to my clients, and racked my brain trying to think of what Gail had said or done to lead Mario to this conclusion. When Mario told me that Gail had this way of holding her head when she got stubborn, I was again baffled by how little it took to create such a strong reaction. Either this couple knew each other extremely well or they were reading things into their communication that were wrong.

I explained to Gail and Mario that they were probably right 60 percent of the time, but that I could help them improve their relationship by 40 percent if they were willing to simply point out what they had noticed to their partner and ask if their conclusion was right or wrong. I also told them that when they stopped their communication in midstream in the belief that they were not being listened to, then they were ensuring the worst possible outcome. By not finishing their thoughts, they were making it truly impossible for their partner to hear their point of view. If they wanted to convince me that they were serious about wanting to be responded to, I was going to make each of them responsible for finishing their statements.

My prediction of how well this couple really knew what the other was feeling was quite accurate, but by learning to finish their statements and check their assumptions with each other, the couple started to slow down their reactions. The times when they were reassured that they were being listened to made it possible for Gail and Mario to realize that they were each equally committed to improving the relationship, which in turn provided a foundation of hope that things could improve.

Flexibility

Few parents feel that they were adequately prepared for the most important and demanding role of their lives. Despite the hours of instruction and coaching that are provided for childbirth, most parents feel totally on their own after the big event. Balancing marriage, children, jobs, and religious and community commitments takes energy, patience, and flexibility.

Parents who are able to work together for the sake of their family learn the importance of resilience and flexibility. Instead of blaming each other when there is an "emergency" or sudden change in plans, they are able to shift gears and take on the task at hand. Their willingness to make adjustments is a wonderful asset not only to their parenting but also to their marriage. For when both partners are able to demonstrate their commitment through actions that involve compromise or sacrifice, their acts of love are rarely taken for granted.

Flexibility also means that partners are open to alternatives and are willing to expand their way of thinking. Partners who do not need to rigidly cling to their beliefs or preferences are not threatened when their spouse suggests an alternate approach; instead they are willing to expand their viewpoint and consider ideas that may never have occurred to them. Many feel blessed that their partner's interests and life experiences can balance areas that are unknown or underdeveloped in their own lives.

When children are raised in an environment where parents are receptive to each other's opinions, they are spared the tension and blame that is inevitable when there is only one "correct" path. The willingness to explore options and consider alternatives usually extends to the children as well, so that each child feels freer to pursue his or her own interests rather than follow rigid expectations where individuality cannot be tolerated.

Forgiveness

Despite good intentions, partners often disappoint or hurt each other. Partners who are able to talk to each other when this happens and then let go of their anger have a wonderful advantage in life. Too many couples that I see in therapy hold on to every disappointment or grievance in a way that only adds to their sense of unhappiness. Partners who do this seem to be searching for comfort through self-righteousness. They cling to the idea that they were wronged or treated unfairly and use this to justify withdrawing or counterattacking. They assume that their partner is an enemy who has not only injured them once, but would undoubtedly hurt them again if allowed to. Unfortunately, their inability to allow their partner to set things right turns a blemish into a scar.

Knowing how to forgive is an active effort that requires an ability to trust and a belief that the good can be restored. It can only happen when the partner who has been aggrieved can bring his or her hurt to the partner who, in turn, must take responsibility for having caused the pain. The ability to work together to resolve the issue and then bring intimacy back into the relationship gives the goodness in the marriage an opportunity to prevail. When spouses do not know how to forgive, past pains accumulate and eventually lead to a defensive posture and distance.

The spirit of trust in parents who know how to forgive adds a wonderful dimension to the entire family. Because they believe in their partner's good intentions and ability to change, there is an air of confidence. Forgiving a partner is truly an act of love and is the only way to create a clean slate. Parents who can give this gift to each other can also give it to their children, for children are also human and apt to make mistakes. In addition to growing up in an environment of trust and acceptance, children who are able to see their parents forgive in an effort to mend their relationship learn the importance of perseverance and the goodness that two people can create.

The Energy to Work on the Positives

While we are all influenced by our past, it is too easy to passively accept negative characteristics and ways of relating that have been passed on or created from earlier experiences. The good qualities that enhance a marriage and create the kind of experience we hope our children will have are available to every parent—but they may require action and change. And although most spouses can imagine how much happier they would be if their partner learned new ways of relating, in order for the positives to take over, the change should ideally include both partners. For most, this involves making a decision to try something new and take a risk. But choosing to build on the good aspects of a marriage has positive consequences that reverberate through the marriage and onto the children. Affection, appreciation, flexibility, friendship, forgiveness, laughter, open-mindedness—when all of these ingredients are added together, they create a family environment that is warm, relaxed, and playful. Children not only escape from the tension and hostility that dominates unhappy marriages but also develop a blueprint of marriage that leads them to anticipate and get the best.

QUESTIONS

1. What quality of your marriage do you prize the most? What needs to happen in your relationship to bring this into the forefront? What diminishes it? What is the next most important strength of your marriage? How often do you get to experience it? What events diminish it?

2. Think about three marriages you have been exposed to in your life (your parents' or your siblings' or friends' marriages). What qualities do you admire the most? How easy or difficult do you think it would be to build that strength into your own marriage?

3. If you were to imagine your marriage as a seesaw with tension and conflict on one side and warmth and friendship on the other, what would your marriage look like?

4. What do you most respect about your partner as a parent? As a spouse? As a person? When was the last time you told him or her how much you appreciated this characteristic?

5. How many times per week do you and your partner hug or hold hands? Who initiates this most of the time? How was affection displayed in your parents' marriage? In your in-laws' marriage? Which relationship does yours most closely resemble when it comes to expressing affection?

9
Building a Better Marriage

"It Is Never Too Late to Try"

It the beginning of this book I explained that some of the chapters would be easy to read, as they would offer confirmation that what is going on in your own marriage is good for you and for your children. However, there are probably one or two areas that may not be going as smoothly as you would like. While you may not have thought about these danger zones too much before, now that you realize the extent to which the children are affected by your marriage you may feel more committed to working on these issues. Although marital therapists can be useful when a couple hits an impasse, you may find that these suggestions can help you begin to make the changes you want.

Imagine the Marriage You Want

When I work with couples, I usually ask them to imagine what their life would be like if the therapy were successful. I ask them to be as specific as possible, and to visualize a scene that would represent the kind of marriage they really want. This becomes the "big picture." It is a goal that is attainable only when both partners keep it in sight. When things get off track, or revert back to an unhappy state, thinking about the way things could be can provide motivation. When partners seem stuck or unable to think of different ways of relating, I ask them to consider what the result will be if they continue doing exactly what they are doing now. I then ask them to compare that image to the vision of what their marriage could be. While finding a different way of handling a situation is not easy or automatic, having a vision of the end result can often make a big difference.

Become More Self-Aware

Having a vision of change provides direction and motivation, but there are other steps that need to be taken in order to get from here to there. Many times our wish for a happy life or a perfect marriage makes it hard to stay with feelings that suggest the opposite. Although most people find it easy to recognize anger, the subtle but persistent signals that surface when important issues are not fully resolved are equally important to tune in to. Partners who avoid discussing certain subjects are often pessimistic that they can solve their problems, and that in a certain sense they have given up. Distance between partners is a symptom of a loss of goodwill or trust and should be taken very seriously. Becoming aware is truly the first step toward improvement.

Self-awareness does not only mean becoming aware of our actions, it also requires that we learn to identify and understand our feelings. Many people have never learned how to tolerate sad or difficult feelings, and may find themselves becoming anxious or very uncomfortable once these feelings have surfaced. In many ways, it takes courage to stay with and discover our innermost selves. Remember, feelings are just feelings; their existence does not mean that something terrible is about to happen.[1] They are also finite. Many people turn away from an emotional experience because they believe the level of discomfort will keep magnifying and don't realize that they have already reached the maximum state of discomfort. Their problem is that they don't know what to do next. While the change process can only begin by acknowledging feelings, once awareness is established there are other steps you can take that will help you feel better.

In order to stay with uncomfortable feelings long enough to understand them, you may need to learn how to soothe yourself. When your children have a bad dream and jump into your arms, they want to be held and comforted. By telling them not to worry and reassuring them that everything will be okay, you give them the strength to return to their beds. Adults also need to be soothed and comforted when anxiety begins to take over. Remind yourself that your bad feelings are just feelings; they can't really hurt you. Taking deep breaths and returning to the big picture for inspiration can help as well. Confiding in your partner or a friend can help you tolerate difficult feelings while moving closer to understanding them. It is only by knowing how we feel that we can make the connection between what is wrong and what needs to be changed.

Most people also need to learn how to get beneath their anger. Anger is an important emotion that alerts us to situations that need to be addressed.[2] But if we look underneath the anger, there are other feelings that are often the most important ones to understand. Frequently, anger is stimulated when we feel afraid, hurt, or disappointed. In order to truly set things straight and create the closeness that will benefit the marriage and the children, it is the underlying feelings that need to be talked about and resolved.

Discover Your Tacit Beliefs and Expectations

Understanding the beliefs and assumptions that are connected to the feelings is another important part of improving our situation. In looking at our marriage, part of this understanding comes from recognizing the beliefs and expectations that came from the blueprint of our own parents' marriage, for that is where we learned how relationships work. It is important to keep in mind that our parents' marriage affects us in two equally powerful ways: the identifications that we have tacitly accepted, regardless of their consequences, and the aspects that we disidentified from and have formed reactions against.

Although it can cause anxiety, it is important to know which parts of our parents' marriage act as an inspiration, and which ones make us wince with discomfort. Not knowing does not spare us from their influence. In fact, the opposite is usually true: When the ghosts from the past invade us in silent ways, we are simply reactive and not able to either maximize the potential strengths or challenge the parts that cause us the most misery. Many of our identifications exist without being fully acknowledged or utilized. In fact, most people have aspects of their parents' marriage that they hold dear and could choose to turn to for strength if they were better understood. Memories of times when parents worked well together or showed their affection can inspire us if we can acknowledge their importance.

Understanding which aspects of our parents' marriage were engraved in our schema can also help us understand our disappointments when our current reality and our blueprint don't match. One example from my own life is how strongly both of my parents acted as caretakers for each other. I remember the first time my mother drove the car on the highway to visit her own parents, who lived a hundred miles away. My father had, of course, filled up the car with gasoline and checked the oil and tire pressure, but he also spent twenty minutes giving my mother advice on how to handle passing cars on the highway, and a detailed map of the exits and directions. Needless to say, my mother had made that trip hundreds of times as a passenger and was an excellent driver, but my father's love for her was clearly communicated that day. Without realizing it, I believed that my husband's willingness to keep the car filled with gas and to offer help in navigating new situations was a statement of love, and that his failure to deliver was surely a sign that he no longer cared about me. Only by recognizing my profound disappointment could I move into the next step of questioning the beliefs and conclusions that had led to my emotional state.

At the end of each chapter, I have provided a list of questions to stimulate awareness of your own beliefs. In addition to thinking about your initial responses, you might also want to maximize this experience by talking to brothers and sisters, looking at childhood pictures, and even stopping to take a fresh look at how your parents interact today. What often happens by talking about our impressions and memories in more depth is the chance to revisit childhood experiences from an adult perspective, and to achieve a more sophisticated understanding of what was going on.

For example, several of the people I have talked about in this book were clearly closer to one of their parents. As a result, their view of the other parent and of their parents' marriage was heavily influenced by the preferred parent's perspective. Recognizing the extent to which we have been asked to side with one parent is essential if we are to consider our parents' marriage from a more objective perspective. When this is understood, we can finally give our parents' marriage back to them. It is wonderfully liberating to give up responsibility for fighting our parents' battles and possessing their beliefs. Only then can we become free to create an intimate relationship that reflects our unique selves. One person who was able to do this was Helen.

Working with Helen

I saw Helen again, several years after she had finished college and was married. She had called me shortly after her father had been hospitalized following a heart attack. As you may recall, Helen had been brought into her parents' marriage as her mother's ally and confidante. She knew everything about her parents' marriage, but only from her mother's perspective. She saw her father as a distant, unresponsive man and marriage as a relationship that provided no support or friendship. In the face of her mother's clear neediness, her father appeared withholding and cruel. When Helen accompanied her mother to the intensive care unit of the hospital, she was shocked by her mother's insistence that her father looked just fine when Helen herself could see that he was unbelievably pale and unresponsive. Fortunately, the heart attack was a relatively mild one, and although her dad needed bed rest and constant monitoring, by the next day he had been moved to a regular room on the cardiac floor. Helen brought her mother to visit shortly after visiting hours began. After about ten minutes, Helen's mom announced that it was disturbing Dad's rest to have all these visitors. She was leaving, and suggested that Helen leave, too. The nurses had not limited visiting time, and the room seemed big and alien. Helen wondered how she would feel staying there alone. Helen thought for a moment and then asked her father if it would be okay for her to stay with him a little longer. He held out his hand for her and smiled gratefully.

When Helen talked with me about this incident, she realized that her mother's view of her father was completely unrealistic. It became obvious to Helen that her mom could not tolerate or even acknowledge her husband's vulnerable side. Yet Helen had few memories of her father ever showing his needy side to anyone. As we talked about different memories from her childhood, Helen could see what her parents' marriage was really all about. Her father had taken on the role of the invincible but withholding partner; her mother, the needy but deprived spouse. By allowing his wife's vulnerable side to flourish and dominate the family, Helen's father had spared himself from knowing his own weaknesses. Yet, in thinking it over, Helen came to the conclusion that her dad had actually been more deprived than her mom.

This awareness was particularly important, for in her own marriage, Helen had found a partner who reinforced her independence and self-sufficiency. Helen had disidentified with her mother's needy possessiveness and rarely showed or talked about her emotions. Her husband was also a man of action who was skeptical of psychology and preferred facts to feelings. Looking at her parents' marriage from a fresh perspective gave Helen the courage to see how no one in her family had known how to acknowledge emotions or support each other. The hand that had reached out to Helen in the hospital room was a symbol of connection and hope. Helen took this hope back to her own marriage, and found that when she initiated a conversation that exposed her confused and vulnerable side, her husband was able to offer her support without scorning her or turning away. It was a new facet of the relationship for both of them, and could never have been reached until Helen became free of the burdens and beliefs of her parents' marriage.

Consider Gender-Based Assumptions

Most of the themes outlined in this book demonstrate the degree to which expectations and behavior are influenced by gender-based expectations. So many of our actions are based on beliefs that were formed by learning from our parents' marriage what happens between men and women. When we look more closely, we may find that the visions that were imprinted are shallow and restrictive. Often they lead to beliefs and expectations that take us far away from who we truly are and what we truly want.

Gender-determined beliefs are so subtle and so deeply ingrained as "normal" behavior that they can be difficult to see. When there is unspoken resentment, hostility, or distance in a marriage, then there are probably important issues that have not been satisfactorily negotiated. Rather than point an accusatory finger at your spouse, it is more important to look inward and think about the style and expectations you have for yourself. Women who do so may find that they are uncomfortable asserting themselves, or that they typically back down when they experience their partner's disapproval or anger. Men who look inward may find that they move too quickly away from feelings or work to find solutions without fully understanding themselves or their partner. Only by acknowledging our own role in perpetuating the dynamics that lead to unhappiness can we consider the next steps that can be taken toward change.

Be Open to New Explanations

Over the years I have come to appreciate the power of beliefs in facilitating change. How we react to a situation is completely dependent on the underlying beliefs that have led us to interpret events in a specific way. One way of experiencing ourselves and our relationship differently is to challenge our assumptions and conclusions. In so doing we become open to the positives and more free to imagine and create the changes we want.

One husband I worked with had a dismissive attitude toward feelings when I first met him. He completely bought into a "macho" stance and by being tough and rational had cut himself off from his feelings. Of course he was also made uncomfortable by his wife's feelings, and would abruptly end conversations when they became "too emotional." In our work, I was able to help him get in touch with a side of himself that he had rarely acknowledged and find the strength to build a relationship that he wanted.

RICHARD AND MOLLY

Richard and Molly had been married for eleven years when they called me for a consultation. Molly's first words to me were, "If it weren't for the children we'd be divorced, but I'm not sure it's worth staying together because things have gotten so bad." Richard, in a reserved but troubled way, added that he had tried everything he knew, but that Molly had simply shut him out of her life. The couple rarely went out together or made love. Each was devoted to their three school-age children, but they usually disagreed on how to raise them and run the house. As a result, there was frequent bickering in front of the children, and sometimes arguments that led to Richard's shouting or walking out.

I asked the couple if things had always been tense and conflictual between them. Molly answered that it used to be just the opposite. "When we met, my mother was dying from cancer. Richard was always there for me, always calm, and always attentive. He was my rock. I don't think I could have gotten through it without him." Surprised, I asked Molly if she had any idea when things had changed.

Molly: I can tell you exactly. Emily is five now. When I was pregnant with her, Richard Junior was four and Scott was two. I had pregnancy-related asthma. The doctors said it would go away after the baby was born, but there wasn't any medication I could take. It was terrible; sometimes I just couldn't breathe.

J.S.: Go on.

Molly: One morning I had a bad attack. Richard was helping with the kids, but it kept getting worse. I thought I was going to die. Then Richard said he had an important meeting at work and he had to leave. I was alone with two kids, I couldn't breathe . . . and he walked out on me!

J.S.: Can you remember what you were thinking?

Molly: He left me to die! I knew then that he didn't really love me. You don't love somebody and walk out on them like that.

I looked at Richard and asked him if he remembered that morning. Answering in a flat, matter-of-fact way, as if giving me directions to the nearest highway entrance, he said:

Richard: Molly had neighbors she could call, or she could go to the emergency room. If I lost my job, the whole family would suffer, and I had an obligation to my business responsibilities.

J.S.: I'm curious about Molly's description of you when you two were dating. She called you her rock. You strike me as a very competent man. Can you talk to me about that?

Richard: I would say practical, but competent is probably okay. I like to think of myself as having a clear head.

J.S.: Were you always like that? Were you a serious kind of kid?

Richard: Not always. I have four brothers, and we were always playing around. But we lived on a farm and there were chores as well. I was the eldest, so I probably was the most serious.

J.S.: What was it like to grow up on a farm?

Richard: Different. We spent much more time together as a family than people do around here. We played and swam, but we didn't need lessons. My mom didn't drive, so we couldn't have gotten to lessons anyway.

J.S.: Do you think your mom ever worried . . . having five kids and not being able to drive in case of an emergency?

Richard: Seven. I have two younger sisters as well. We had a lot of land, so there were no close neighbors. I think my mom just didn't let us have any problems. She never fussed much when we were sick, and anything that needed a car had to wait till my dad got home. Frankly, I don't remember having any problems.

J.S.: Well, as the eldest of seven kids, isolated on a farm with no driver most of the time, I can see how you became responsible. You had to learn how to cope with all kinds of things on your own. I can see how Molly said you were her "rock." Was your father a rock to your mother as well?

Richard: Both my parents are "no-nonsense" kind of people. They worked hard and were busy keeping the farm going. My mother did her part, and my father did his.

J.S.: Molly, I'm starting to think about Richard's being a rock, and how important that is to both of you. What if Richard believes that you can only love the part of him that is strong . . . the part that is the rock? What if Richard wasn't feeling like a rock the morning you had your asthma attack? What if he was as frightened as you were?

Molly: You mean, what if Richard was scared when I had my attack?

J.S. (looking toward Richard): I can't imagine what it felt like to be watching my wife gasp for air and not know how to help her.

Richard (with tears in his eyes): I was scared. I can't believe that I ran away, but I couldn't take it.

Molly: Richard, I had no idea that you were scared. You never tell me about your feelings. I always think that you don't have any.

J.S.: Molly, would it seem different to you if you believed that Richard thought you could only love the part of him that was the "rock" . . . that if he showed you his weak side you wouldn't respect him or love him?

Molly: That he didn't leave that day because he didn't love me? He just couldn't handle it?

At that point in our session, Molly got sad and reflective. She started to cry, and said to Richard, "It would make a big difference."

In our next session, I worked with Richard's need to see himself as a rock, and his obvious discomfort with feelings. Richard had always seen himself as being competent, and took this role in the marriage. As we began to think about his life on the farm, Richard began to realize that neither of his parents had any time or the ability to listen to his feelings. Richard also recognized that there was a belief system about competency in his family, and that the fact that his mother couldn't drive was a source of humiliation. His silent, stoic father had played the role of "rock" in his marriage, but had never exposed his own weaknesses or vulnerabilities. As we talked about feelings, Richard admitted that he often felt anxious, but that he had learned to switch off this experience by getting very busy.

When I asked Richard and Molly to create their "big picture" of the marriage they wished to have, there was some confusion. Although Molly's first impulse was to want things to return to the way they had been before the kids were born, she could see that the formula of "Richard as rock" would never bring them the happiness she wanted. After some discussion, Richard decided that what he really wanted was a marriage in which he could feel respected and welcomed, and Molly wanted a marriage in which they could really talk together about what they were feeling. If Richard thought that Molly could respect him for sharing his vulnerable side, then he was ready to try it. In a trial run in my office, Richard started to tell Molly about the pressure he was under at work. At first, talking about feelings was noticeably uncomfortable for him. Richard had to fight his expectation that Molly would think less of him, and his own discomfort in acknowledging that there were things in his life that were not perfect. At one point, Richard turned to me and said, "I used to think it took strength to keep things inside and handle everything on my own. Now I know that what really takes strength is finding the courage to stick with your feelings and say them out loud."

Seeing his ability to know and expose his vulnerable side as a strength empowered Richard to take risks and continue with this process. As Richard soon discovered, talking out his feelings helped him become calmer, and when Molly was able to listen and offer him support and respect, the bond between them blossomed.

Until she was able to consider that Richard's walking out on her had been a sign of being overwhelmed rather than a statement of not loving her, Molly could not forgive him or make herself vulnerable again. Until Richard was able to see that working with his feelings took courage and reflected strength rather than weakness, he could not become involved in the relationship in the way both partners truly wanted. If there is such a thing as a recipe for change, it begins with a vision of a better life and an awareness of the issues that are obstacles to better ways of relating. Change is much easier when you can challenge the beliefs that have kept things in place. When we can see how the story of our marriage is based on assumptions and interpretations that may be limiting or incorrect, we may become more open to a different perspective.

Become a Team

Of course, change is much easier when both parties are participating. In order to accomplish this, communication is a vital part of the process. When partners can work together to understand their relationship and the belief system that is in place, then even the process of achieving awareness can generate closeness. When I work with couples, I stress the importance of working together. I emphasize how important it is that they become a team in order to strengthen their marriage and lead their family. To me, a team is committed to a shared goal and objective. It is easier to compromise and give support when you both want the same thing and are working equally hard to achieve it. When partners are on the same side again, the details of how things should change become much more feasible.

Team members know that protecting each other makes it possible for the team to succeed. When I work with couples who are highly reactive to each other or who tend to get into repetitive patterns of "old" unresolved issues, I try to help them understand the sequence from a new perspective. Typically, one partner has moved into an overreactive position while the other still has some semblance of being grounded. If that partner could appreciate that for one brief moment he or she has an option and an opportunity to help their spouse get back on track, many serious arguments and painful interactions could be averted. Instead of taking the bait and jumping in with the response that has been provoked, it is possible to respond in a way that is calming and nonreactive. There is no question that this is challenging to do, and yet we somehow find the strength to do it for our children. Parents who are able to experiment with ways of using their strength to help their partner in this way often discover that the rewards are well worth it.

Separate the Past from the Present

Another way of helping to strengthen your marriage comes from learning to distinguish old hurts and disappointments from the reality of the here and now. Our cognitive maps are very powerful, as they not only guide the way we interpret situations and arrive at conclusions but they also control our emotional state and expectation of what comes next. When an interaction between partners is similar to an unhappy childhood experience, too often the entire meaning structure from the past is activated. At that point, all of our intense feelings and beliefs from childhood flood the stage and get commingled with the immediate situation. Old beliefs and expectations similarly get reawakened and distort our understanding and reactions.

Once a person realizes the specific themes from the past that tend to get stimulated and overpower the present, he or she is more able to identify the process when it starts. By knowing how old schemas can distort conclusions and provoke overwhelming feelings it is possible to stop the cycle from building. Change is accomplished by reminding ourselves that the present is not the past. Being able to distinguish and contrast the two experiences helps allow the old wounds to stay in the background, which enables us to focus more accurately on the situation at hand.

Use the Power of Accountability and Forgiveness

Anger that is clung to is one of the most damaging forces in a marriage. Whether it simmers beneath the surface, erupts in periodic episodes of rage, or is displayed in daily expressions of hostility and resentment, it creates a caustic environment for parents and children. While anger serves a purpose in alerting us to situations that need to be addressed, it should be viewed as an invitation to action. When spouses create lists of grievances, they are adding to a belief system that prevents them from trusting, sharing with, and enjoying their partner. If the good in the marriage is ever to prevail, grievances must be handled in a more constructive way.

A marriage can be greatly improved when partners are able to talk to each other about something that has troubled or upset them. There are many self-help books that address the ways in which partners can approach this subject constructively, including being specific about the primary concern rather than bringing up a string of injuries at one time, and by speaking calmly and respectfully rather than insulting or provoking your partner.[3] But it is equally important for each of you to know how to accept responsibility when you have created the injury. Even if it was unintentional, or if you think your partner is overreacting, the incident can only be forgiven if you admit your part in causing the hurt. Even something as simple as "I didn't realize that this would bother you so much; I never intended to hurt you" goes a long way in letting your partner know that his or her feelings have been heard and validated.

But the incident is not fully resolved until it can be forgiven. Learning to accept an apology and trust in a partner's sincerity is necessary in order to move beyond a self-protective stance that ultimately adds to marital distance and perpetuates anger. Forgiveness in response to a partner's accountability is a magical formula in reestablishing love and connection. It is not only a tonic for the marriage, but for the children, who can witness a constructive way to handle conflict and disappointment, and who are the ones who have the most to benefit from a relaxed, conflict-free home.

For the Sake of Our Children

Even though I am a marriage therapist and know a great deal about human behavior, some of what I learned when researching this book shocked me into taking a closer look at my own marriage. I thought about all the times I had fought with my husband in front of the kids, and the times I had been angry and put my husband down in their presence. There have even been times when I have put our children in the middle. While not all vows are taken seriously, I have certainly made my own pledge to do things differently—for the sake of my children.

If I want my children to feel confident and proud of themselves, then I must commit to holding back comments about their father that are sarcastic or disrespectful. If I want my children to believe in the safety of marriage, I must be careful to control my temper and think carefully before snapping out in anger. In writing this book, I became aware of several "old" issues that I had not fully resolved with my husband, but that rankled inside, creating pessimism and resentment. The past few months have been interesting around our home; I can assure you that there have been many conversations that might not otherwise have occurred.

But when I look at my children's faces, I feel good about the risks I have taken and the moments of tension that occurred when difficult issues were reawakened. I know I have done something of value—not only for myself and my relationship with my husband, but for the future of our children. I am closer to realizing the picture that I envision for my own happy marriage, and hopeful that by strengthening this bond I am giving something precious to my children—the legacy of positive lessons of love.

QUESTIONS

1. When you think about the parts of your marriage that are similar to your parents' marriage, what do you most highly value? What do you wish was different?

2. If you could have magically changed your parents' relationship, what would you have done? If the magic had worked, would any part of your life be different?

3. What problems or situations are likely to get connected to bigger issues from the past? Do you know what these "tender" issues are for your partner?

4. How easily does your partner calm down when you are able to stay calm? Does your partner know the best way to reach you when you have started to overreact to something?

5. Are there times when you feel trapped by old decisions that no longer reflect who you are or what you really want? When was the last time you tried to talk about this with your partner?

6. If you were to imagine how your "dream" marriage would be five years from now, how close are you to realizing it? Can you think of two ways of being that would happen often in your dream marriage? How would your partner react if you were to try being that way now?

Notes

Chapter One: How Children Learn from the Marriage

1. To learn more about social learning theory, the reader can refer to Bandura and Walters, *Social Learning and Personality Development* (1963).
2. Several research studies have looked at the way cognitive structure affects perception. See, for example, Baucom, Epstein, Sayers, and Sher (1989), p. 31. Also see Dobson and Kendall (1993), p. 8, and Chelune, Robison, and Kommor (1984), p. 19.
3. For an excellent summary of Piaget's work, see Hugh Rosen (1985). The experiment described here appears on p. 15.
4. Bernstein, A. Quoted by Mary F. Whiteside (1986), p. 156.
5. Neisser (1994), p. 6.

6. Lewis and Owen (1995), p. 462.
7. Hampson, Hyman, and Beavers (1994), pp. 66–67.
8. Robins, Schoenberg, Holmes, et al. (1985), p. 37.
9. Langston, p. 128.
10. The process of identification has been explained particularly well by W. Meissner (1986), p. 240.
11. Snyder, Velasquez, and Clark (1997), p. 192.
12. Fuss (1995), p. 6.
13. Quoted from Josselson (1996), p. 145.
14. Gerson and Hoffman (1993), p. 341.
15. David and Jill Scharff were the first to discuss the "internalized couple" in their book *Object Relations Family Therapy* (1987), p. 241.
16. The repetition of dynamics is a subject that I have discussed in professional papers and books. See Siegel (1991), p. 72, and Siegel (1992), pp. 9–19. See also Scarf (1986), p. 126.
17. James Framo first wrote about this in a journal article titled "Symptoms from a family transactional viewpoint" (1970), p. 128. The role of children in stabilizing their parents' marriage appears in Byng-Hall (1980), p. 356. Also see Scarf (1986).
18. See also Ackerman (1986).
19. The term "enmeshment," developed by Minuchin, is well described by Gerson (1996), pp. 140–142.
20. Edward Waring (1980), p. 474, reported that the happiest couples in his research study said that their parents' successful marriage PROFOUNDLY affected their own marital success.
21. Steil (1997).

Chapter Two: Establishing the Priority of the Marriage

1. Neuman (1998), p. 93, cites this divorce rate based on the U.S. Census Bureau: National Center for Health Statistics. The high incidence of unhappy marriages that do not end in divorce but are not responsive to marital therapy has been discussed by Heaton and Albrecht (1991), p. 747. Research on the relationship between

depression amd marital problems is cited in Prince and Jacobson (1995), p. 380.

2. This theme has also been stressed by Wallerstein (1996). See also Weeks (1995), pp. 37–39, and Taffel (1994), p. 231.

3. Carter and McGoldrick (1989), p. 15.

4. Falicov (1998), p. 38, describes how intimacy between marital partners and others varies in different cultures.

5. Stierlin and Weber (1989), p. 31.

6. Harkaway (1989), p. 236.

7. Josselson (1996), p. 162.

8. Swidler (1980), p. 128.

9. Barnes (1990), p. 223.

10. Stiver (1991), p. 158.

11. Brody, Pillegrini, and Sigel (1986), p. 291. Also see Kerig (1993), p. 29.

12. Three studies that provide important information about the adjustment to having children are those done by Mackey and O'Brien (1995), Cowan and Cowan (1992), and Belsky and Rovine (1990).

13. Taffel (1995), p. 32.

14. Mackay and O'Brien (1995) reported that three years after the first child was born, 10 percent of the study's white American couples were divorced and 6 percent had separated. The black American couples in their study had a higher rate of marriage dissolution, with 24 percent having divorced and 17 percent living separately. Similar rates were reported by Crohan (1996), p. 936.

15. Belsky and Kelly (1994), p. 134.

16. Westfall (1995), p. 180. Also see Spring (1996), p. 139.

17. Cowan and Cowan (1992), p. xi.

18. Sabatelli and Anderson (1991), p. 363.

Chapter Three: Teaching the Value of Interdependence

1. Waring (1983), p. 48. See also Beavers (1985), pp. 75–83.

2. Josselson (1996).

3. See, for example, Levant (1998).

4. This is especially well described by Hafner (1986) in chapter two, "Sex-Role Stereotyping and Conflict," pp. 16–46.

5. Hare-Mustin (1994), p. 19. See also Worden and Worden (1998), pp. 5–9, and Sheinberg and Penn (1991), p. 34.

6. Krystal (1988), pp. 258–263.

7. Lerner (1989), p. 204. See also Stiver (1991), p. 155.

8. Josselson (1987), p. 230.

9. Stiver (1991), p. 160.

10. McQuillan and Ferree (1998), pp. 215–216, studied 230 couples and found that when a wife feels understood by her husband, both husbands and wives have higher levels of satisfaction with their relationship. Similarly, wives who said that it was very easy to raise issues with their husbands came from marriages in which both spouses reported more satisfaction. See also Heller and Wood (1998), p. 273.

11. Mackey and O'Brien (1995).

12. Levant (1997), p. 441.

13. In this research project, fifty-six families with a preschool child were studied when the children were five, and again when they were eight. The findings are presented in Hooven, Gottman, and Katz (1995), p. 229, and Gottman (1998), p. 174.

14. Whitbourne and Ebmeyer (1990), p. 25.

15. Loewenstein (1967), p. 798.

16. Larson, Hammond, and Harper (1998), p. 498.

17. Citing studies from Cox (1989), Howes and Markman (1989), and Zeanah, Borris, and Larrieu (1997), p. 174, report that closeness between marital partners is associated with sensitive parental caregiving and with secure infant attachment.

Chapter Four: Instilling the Importance of Mutual Respect

1. Kohut's theories about self-esteem are presented in several books and articles, including *The Analysis of the Self* (New York: Interna-

tional Universities Press, 1971) and *The Restoration of the Self* (New York: International Universities Press, 1977). His ideas have also been captured in Alice Miller's book *Prisoners of Childhood* (New York: Basic Books, 1981).

Chapter Five: Maintaining Trust in Word and Deed

1. Chelune, Robinson, and Kommor (1984), p. 31.
2. For excellent presentations of the challenges involved in blended families, see Bray (1998). See also Hetherington and Jodl (1994), p. 57.
3. Hansky (1981). See also Siegel (1992), p. 42.
4. The "obsessing" dynamic is described well by Brown (1991), pp. 74–78. Also see Westfall (1989), p. 169.
5. Scanzoni (1984), p. 26.
6. Brown (1991), pp. 246–249.
7. Ibid., p. 273.
8. Wallerstein and Blakeslee (1989), p. 22.
9. Spring (1996), p. 127.
10. Gottman (1998), p. 177, cites recent census bureau statistics that show the percentages of children living in nuclear families (with two parents) to be: 56 percent of white American children, 38 percent of Hispanic-American children, and 26 percent of African-American children.
11. Neuman (1998), p. 93, reports that half the children from divorced homes haven't seen their noncustodial parent in the past year, and that only one in six has weekly contact. Neuman calculates that this is a reality for approximately 20 million American children.
12. Duran-Aydintug (1997) reports that in a sample of sixty university students whose parents were divorced, 82 percent said that they did not trust their current partner. A similar theme is reported by Thornton and Freedman (1982), p. 302.
13. Lee (1995), p. 62.
14. Berner (1992) reports that the commitment to parenting is particu-

larly strong among parents whose parents were divorced, pp. 73–80.

15. The higher divorce rates among adults whose parents were divorced have been cited in several studies. However, as Kulka and Weingarten (1979), p. 68, point out, the differences are also reduced when education at the time of marriage is factored into the equation.
16. Timmer, Veroff, and Hatchett (1996), p. 336.
17. Mackey and O'Brien (1995).
18. While the original studies of the consequences of divorce for children looked at issues such as stigma (see for example, Glenn [1985], p. 69), more recent studies suggest that adverse symptoms are most likely to occur when there have been high levels of conflict or when children are brought into the middle. For example, Buchanan, Maccoby, and Dornbusch (1991), p. 1015, interviewed 522 adolescents four years after their parents had separated. Kids who said they felt caught between conflicted parents had problems such as headaches, depression, eating disorders, exhaustion, and anxiety. See also Thornton and Freedman (1982), p. 302; Kozuch and Cooney (1995), p. 58; and Lee (1995), p. 63. See Amato, Loomis, and Booth (1995), p. 895.
19. Gottman (1998), p. 180. See also Neuman (1998), p. 93.

Chapter Six: Negotiating Differences Constructively

1. Margolin (1988), p. 195.
2. Krystal (1988), pp. 49–53.
3. In 1988, 28 million children in the United States were estimated to live in homes with alcoholic parents according to Gotlib and Avison (1993), p. 296. Straussner (1994), p. 394, suggests that almost 40 percent of adults in the United States have a blood relative with an alcohol problem, which does not take into account the substantial number of children raised by parents who abuse other substances such as cocaine.
4. Gorski (1993), p. 63.

5. Cowan (1997), p. 150.
6. Kerr and Bowen (1988), p. 65.
7. Lerner (1989), p. 294.
8. Harter (1997), p. 83, found that spouses were self-focused, became depressed, and felt less authentic.
9. See Hare-Mustin (1994), p. 34. See also Steil (1997), pp. 27–39; Larson, Hammond, and Harper (1998), p. 488; and Knudson-Martin (1997), p. 423.
10. Rabin (1996), p. 64, writes about the reactions of friends and relatives when her husband quit his job to support her academic sabbatical leave.
11. Steil (1997), p. 29.
12. Scanzoni (1989), p. 81.
13. Schneider (1990), p. 122.
14. See Lachtar (1998) or Siegel (1999).
15. Soncinni (1997), p. 85.
16. Howes and Markman (1989), p. 1050. See also McQuillan and Ferree (1998), p. 216.

Chapter Seven: Understanding the Long-Term Effects of Conflict

1. Cowan and Cowan (1991), pp. 84–85, suggest that women are most unhappy in the first six months postpartum, particularly about assuming greater responsibility for house and child care. Their husbands become more dissatisfied in the following six to eighteen months. Belsky, Belsky, and Rovine (1990), p. 8, have also determined that there was a decline in marital satisfaction after the baby's birth in the 128 couples they studied, from the wife's pregnancy to three years postpartum. The "U-Shape" theory of marital satisfaction is also discussed by Mackey and O'Brien (1995), p. 127, who found that the amount of conflict experienced by white American couples tripled from the prechild to the early child-rearing days. However, the authors suggest that there is also a progressive

side, as many couples make gains in learning to work together.

2. Allen (1996), p. 106.

3. A classic paper written by O'Leary and Arias in 1988 estimated a 25 percent incidence of spouse abuse, pp. 104–127. The National Family Violence Survey cited in McNeal and Amato (1998), p. 123, indicates that more than 3 million children witness inter-parental violence every year. Cassidy (1989), p. 32, interviewed 174 randomly selected families and found that the majority of children had been exposed to extreme parental conflict. Of the 350 children interviewed, 337 had been exposed to verbal or emotional abuse, 121 to parental intimidation, and 93 to parental physical abuse.

4. Wallerstein and Blakeslee (1989), pp. 116–121.

5. The changes in children who are exposed to extreme marital conflict have been documented in numerous studies. The best summary of the research is provided by E. M. Cummings and P. Davies (1994), p. 3, who note that children who have been exposed to marital hostility have extreme behavior problems at a rate that is 600 percent greater than the rate in the general public. Beach (1995), pp. 72 and 102, studied fifth-, sixth-, and seventh-graders and found that children are especially responsive to their mother's use of physical aggression, which resulted in high levels of child aggression, anxiety, depression, somatic complaints, and social difficulties. See also Amato and Keith (1991), p. 38; Grych and Fincham (1990), p. 270; and Cummings, Pellegrini, and Notraius (1989), p. 1040.

6. McNeil and Amato (1998), p. 136, interviewed 471 young adults whose parents were assessed to have had an abusive relationship when were interviewed ten years earlier. The authors found that the majority of these children were now in violent relationships themselves. Also see Amato and Keith (1991), p. 38; Gynch and Fincham (1990), p. 269; and Cappell and Heiner (1990), p. 143.

7. See Belsky and Roving (1981), cited in Katz (1990), pp. 17–20.

8. Howard and Weeks (1995) report that one half of all patients receiving psychiatric treatment sought help because of marital

problems, and that 30 percent of all couples with marital problems have one spouse who is clinically depressed (p. 96). Rusheer and Gotlib also found that depressed patients report more marital discord than do their nondepressed counterparts (cited in Gotlib and Avison [1993], p. 300). Tronsley, Beach, and Fincham (1991), p. 143, suggest that 50 percent of women who are depressed have serious marital problems. Depression makes a parent feel exhausted and easily overwhelmed, less able to play with or enjoy a child, and more likely to withdraw or react to a child with hostility. Also see Guttman (1989), p. 253. See also Anthony (1983), pp. 8–11.

9. Cowan, P. (1997), p. 148.
10. Harold, Fincham, Osborne, and Conger (1997), pp. 347–348.
11. Grych and Fincham (1990), p. 286, reviewed twenty-five studies that show how parental conflict affects children of different ages. Cummings and Davies (1994), pp. 37–86, review both the direct and indirect effects of conflict and explain the dynamics that lead to externalizing behaviors (problems at school, relationship problems with peers, and aggression) versus internalizing behaviors (depression, anxiety, and low self-esteem). Grych (1991) studied 222 children from the fourth and fifth grades and found that the children's exposure to frequent, intense, and poorly resolved marital conflict led to bullying and mean behavior. Cummings and Davies (1994), p. 135, suggest that children who are exposed to frequent background conflict stay in a state of high arousal that reduces their emotional resources and energy. See also Easterbrooks and Emde (1994), pp. 164–165; O'Brien, Bahadur, et al. (1997), p. 39; and Emery (1982), p. 312.
12. Cummings and Davis (1994), p. 40.
13. See Cummings, Pellegrini, and Notarius (1989), pp. 1035–1036. Also see Cummings and Cummings (1988), and Dodge (cited in Grych and Fincham [1990], p. 286).
14. Allen (1996), p. 98, studied the effects of mutually hostile as well as distancing conflict styles. Katz (1990), p. 116, found that children whose parents withdrew when conflict occurred had heightened anger as well as problems regulating their emotions.

15. Schwartz and Zuroff (1979), p. 398, studied ninety-eight college students and found that those who reported parental conflict were more vulnerable to depression. Also see Harold, Fincham, Osborne, and Conger (1997), p. 333, and Howes and Markman (1989), p. 1051.

16. Hoovan, Gottman, and Katz (1995), p. 229. Also see Gohm, Oishi, Darlington, and Diener (1998), p. 319.

17. Amato, Loomis, and Booth (1995), p. 913, examined the consequences of marital conflict in 2,033 adults and their children over a twelve-year period. The researchers were able to determine that children who had escaped a hostile family environment because of their parents' divorce were emotionally better off than those children whose parents remained together and maintained high-level conflict (p. 913). Also see Kulka and Weingarten (1979), p. 50; Kelly (1998), p. 259; Amato and Keith (1991), p. 38; and Gohm, Oishi, et al. (1998), p. 69.

18. Kerig (1995), p. 28, studied seventy-five intact families with a first-born child aged six to ten years. She found that parents involved in cross-generational coalitions were more likely to be dissatisfied with their marriages and have high degrees of marital conflict. Researchers O'Brien, Margolin, and John (1995), p. 3460, interviewed eighty-three families and found that children who became involved in their parents' marital conflict had higher levels of maladjustment.

19. Emery (1982), p. 324. See also Grych (1991), p. 69.

20. Coltrane (1998), p. 206, summarizes research studies showing that fathers enforce gender stereotypes more than do mothers, especially in sons. Pollock (1992) describes how this leads to alienation between father and sons as well as a perpetuation of emotional constriction. See also Levant (1998), p. 441.

21. Cummings and Davies (1994), p. 38, point out that children who witness interparental hostility anticipate that some of the conflict may come their way. Harold, Fincham, Osborne, and Conger (1997) note that marital hostility may indeed lead to a more hostile parent-child relationship. See also Barber (1998), p. 119.

22. Guerin and Gordon (1986), pp. 158–166.
23. Kerig (1995), p. 333.
24. Jurkovic (1997), p. 30.
25. Wallerstein (1989) describes this phenomenon on pp. 60, 63, and 104. Researchers McNeal and Amato (1998), p. 135, have demonstrated that children exposed to marital violence between the ages of eleven and nineteen continue to be affected five to ten years later. See also Kulka and Weingarten (1979), p. 51, and Cappell and Heiner (1990), p. 135.
26. Kendall and Dobson (1993), p. 6.
27. Gottman (1994), p. 110.
28. Easterbrooks (1994), p. 160.
29. Cumming and Davies (1994), pp. 70–78. Also see Grych and Fincham (1990), pp. 285–286.

Chapter Eight: Emphasizing the Positives

1. Gottman (1994), p. 57.
2. Mackey and O'Brien (1995), p. 141.
3. Steil (1997), p. 28.
4. See Beavers (1985), pp. 82 and 165.
5. Noller (1984), p. 22.

Chapter Nine: Building a Better Marriage

1. See Wenning (1998), especially pp. 62–79.
2. Lerner (1985), pp. 100–107.
3. Wenning (1998), pp. 68–77. See also Gottman (1994), pp. 181–199.

Bibliography

Ackerman, Robert. *Growing in the Shadow: Children of Alcoholics*. Pompino Beach, Fla.: Health Communications, 1986.

Ahrons, Constance R. *The Good Divorce*. New York: HarperCollins, 1994.

Aida, Yukie, and Toni Falbo. "Relationships Between Marital Satisfaction, Resources and Power Strategies." *Sex Roles* 24 (1991): 43–55.

Allen, Melissa. *Children's Perceptions and Comparisons of Two Marital Conflict Patterns: Mutually Hostile and Demand-Withdraw*. Doctoral dissertation, Texas A&M University, 1996.

Amato, Paul R., and Bruce Keith. "Parental Divorce and the Well-Being of Children: A Meta-Analysis." *Psychological Bulletin* 110, no. 1 (1991): 26–46.

Amato, Paul R., Laura Spenser Loomis, and Alan Booth. "Parental Divorce, Marital Conflict, and Offspring Well-Being During Early Adulthood." *Social Forces* 73, no. 3 (1995): 895–915.

Ambert, Anne Marie. *Parents, Children and Adolescents: Interactive Relationships and Development in Context.* New York: Haworth, 1997.

Bandura, Albert, and Walters. *Social Learning and Personality Development.* New York: Holt Rinehart & Winston, 1963.

Barber, Brian K. "Interparental Conflict Styles and Youth Problem Behaviors: A Two-Sample Replication Study." *Journal of Marriage and the Family* 60 (1998): 119–132.

Barnes, Gill G. "The Little Woman and the World of Work." In *Gender and Power in Families*, edited by R. J. Perelberg and A. C. Miller, 221–244. New York: Routledge, 1990.

Baucom, Donald H., and Adams. "Assessing Communication in Marital Interaction." In *Assessment of Marital Discord: An Integration for Research and Clinical Practice.* Hillsdale, N.J.: Lawrence Erlbaum, 1987.

Baucom, Donald H., Norman Epstein, Steven Sayers, and Tamara G. Sher. "The Role of Cognitions in Marital Relationships: Definitional, Methodological and Conceptual Issues." *Journal of Consulting and Clinical Psychology* 57 (1989): 31–38.

Beach, Beverly K. *The Relation Between Marital Conflict and Child Adjustment: An Examination of Parental and Child Repertoires.* Doctoral dissertation, West Virginia University, 1995.

Beavers, W. Robert. *Successful Marriage: A Family Systems Approach to Couples Therapy.* New York: W. W. Norton, 1985.

Belsky, Jay, and Michael Rovine. "Patterns of Marital Change Across the Transition to Parenthood: Pregnancy to Three Years Postpartum." *Journal of Marriage and the Family* 52 (1990): 5–19.

Benjamin, Lorna S., and Frances J. Friedrich. "Contributions of Structural Analysis of Social Behavior (SASB) to the Bridge Between Cognitive Science and a Science of Object Relations." In *Person, Schemas and Maladaptive Interpersonal Patterns*, edited by Mardi J. Horowitz. Chicago: University of Chicago Press, 1991.

Berner, R. Thomas. *Parents Whose Parents Were Divorced.* New York: Haworth, 1992.

Bernstein, Ann C. "Stepfamilies with a Mutual Child." Reported in Mary F. Whiteside, "Remarried Systems," in *Children in Family Con-*

texts: Perspectives on Treatment, edited by Lee Combrick-Graham. New York: Guilford, 1986.

Black, Claudia. *It Will Never Happen to Me.* Denver: Medical Administration Corp., 1981.

Booth A., and J. Dunn. *Stepfamilies: Who Benefits? Who Does Not?* Hillsdale, N.J.: Lawrence Erlbaum, 1994.

Bray, James H., and John Kelly. *Stepfamilies: Love, Marriage and Parenting in the First Decade.* New York: Bantam, Doubleday, Dell, 1998.

Brody, Gene H., Anthony D. Pillegrini, and Irving E. Sigel. "Marital Quality and Mother-Child and Father-Child Interactions with School-Aged Children." *Developmental Psychology* 22, no. 3 (1986): 291–296.

Brown, Emily M. *Patterns of Infidelity and Their Treatment.* New York: Brunner/Mazel, 1991.

Buchanan, Christy M., Eleanor E. Maccoby, and Sanford M. Dornbusch. "Caught Between Parents: Adolescents' Experience in Divorced Homes." *Child Development* 62 (1991): 1008–1029.

Burman, Bonnie, Richard S. John, and Gayla Margolin. "Effects of Marital and Parent-Child Relations on Children's Adjustment." *Journal of Family Psychology* 1, no. 1 (1987):91–108.

Byng-Hall, John. "Symptom Bearer as Marital Distance Regulator: Clinical Implications." *Family Process* 19 (1980): 355–365.

Cappell, Charles, and Robert B. Heiner. "The Intergenerational Transmission of Family Aggression." *Journal of Family Violence* 5 (1990): 135–152.

Carli, Linda L. "Gender, Language and Influence." *Journal of Personality and Social Psychology* 59, no. 5 (1990): 941–951.

Carter, Betty, and Monica McGoldrick. "The Changing Family Life Cycle: A Framework for Family Therapy." In *The Changing Family Life Cycle,* second edition, edited by B. Carter and M. McGoldrick, 3–28. Boston: Allyn and Bacon, 1989.

Cassady, M. E. *The Family Responses to Conflict Scale: Development of a Measure of Marital Conflict and Children's Exposure and Reactions.* Doctoral dissertation, University of Connecticut, 1989.

Chelune, Gordon J., Joan T. Robison, and Martin J. Kommor. "A Cognitive Interactional Model of Intimate Relationships." In *Commu-*

nication, Intimacy, and Close Relationships, edited by Steve Duck. New York: Academic Press, 1984.

Christensen, Andrew, and Christopher L. Heavey. (1990). "Gender and Social Structure in the Demand/Withdraw Pattern of Marital Conflict." *Journal of Personality and Social Psychology* 59, no. 1 (1990): 73–81.

Clulow, Christopher, ed. *Partners Becoming Parents*. Northvale, N.J.: Jason Aronson, 1997.

Coltrane, Scott. "Gender, Power and Emotional Expression: Social and Historical Contexts for a Process Model of Men in Marriages and Families." In *Men in Families*, edited by Alan Booth and Ann C. Crouter, 193–211. Mahwah, N.J.: Lawrence Erlbaum, 1998.

Cowan, Carolyn P., and Phillip A. Cowan. *When Partners Become Parents: The Big Life Change for Couples*. New York: Basic Books, 1992.

Cowan, Carolyn P., Phillip A. Cowan, Gertrude Heming, Ellen Garrett, William S. Coysh, Harriet Curtis-Boles, and Abner Boles, III. "Transitions to Parenthood: His, Hers and Theirs." *Journal of Family Issues* 6, no. 4 (1985): 451–481.

Cowan, Phillip A. "Being Partners: Effects on Parenting and Child Development." In *Partners Becoming Parents*, edited by Christopher Clulow, 140–158. Northvale, N.J.: Jason Aronson, 1997.

Cowan, Phillip A., and E. Mavis Hetherington. *Family Transitions*. Hillsdale, N.J.: Lawrence Erlbaum, 1991.

Cox, Martha J., Margaret T. Owen, Jerry M. Lewis, and V. Kay Henderson. "Marriage, Adult Adjustment and Early Parenting." *Child Development* 60 (1989): 1015–1024.

Cox, Martha J., Margaret T. Owen, Jerry M. Lewis, Cynthia Riedel, Lynda Scalf-McIver, and Ana Suster. "Intergenerational Influences on the Parent-Infant Relationship in the Transition to Parenthood." *Journal of Family Issues* 6, no. 4 (1985): 543–564.

Crohan, Susan E. "Marital Quality and Conflict Across the Transition to Parenthood in African American and White Couples." *Journal of Marriage and the Family* 58 (1996): 933–944.

Crohn, Joel. "Intercultural Couples." In *Re-visioning Family Therapy: Face, Culture and Gender in Clinical Practice*, edited by Monika McGoldrick, 295–308. New York: Guilford, 1998.

Cummings, E. Mark, and Patrick Davies. *Children and Marital Conflict: The Impact of Family Dispute and Resolution.* New York: Guilford, 1994.

Cummings, Jennifer S., David S. Pellegrini, Clifford I. Notarious, and E. Mark Cummings. "Children's Responses to Angry Adult Behavior as a Function of Marital Distress and History of Interparent Hostility." *Child Development* 60 (1989): 1035–1043.

David, Corrine, Ric Steele, Rex Forehand, and Lisa Armistead. "The Role of Family Conflict and Marital Conflict in Adolescent Functioning." *Journal of Family Violence* 11, no. 1 (1996): 81–91.

Dobson, Keith, and Philip C. Kendall, eds. *Psychopathology and Cognition.* New York: Academic Press, 1993.

Duran-Aydintug, Candan. "Adult Children of Divorce Revisited: When They Speak Up." *Journal of Divorce & Remarriage* 27, nos. 1 and 2 (1997): 71–83.

Easterbrooks, M. Ann, E. Mark Cummings, and Robert N. Emde. "Young Children's Responses to Constructive Marital Disputes." *Journal of Family Psychology* 8, no. 2 (1994): 160–169.

Emery, Robert D. "Interparental Conflict and the Children of Discord and Divorce." *Psychological Bulletin* 92 (1982): 310–330.

Falicov, Celia J. "The Cultural Meaning of Family Triangles." In *Re-Visioning Family Therapy: Face, Culture and Gender in Clinical Practice,* edited by Monika McGoldrick, 33–49. New York: Guilford, 1998.

Framo, James. "Symptoms from a Family Transactional Viewpoint." *Family Therapy in Transition,* edited by Nathan Ackerman, 125–170. Boston: Little Brown, 1970.

Freedman, Jill, and Gene Combs. *Narrative Therapy: The Social Construction of Preferred Realities.* New York: Norton, 1996.

Fuss, Diane. *Identification Papers.* London: Routledge, 1995.

Gable, Sara, Keith Cernic, and Jay Belsky. "Coparenting Within the Family System: Influences on Children's Development. *Family Relations* 43 (1994): 380–386.

Gerson, Mary-Joan. *The Embedded Self: A Psychoanalytic Guide to Family Therapy.* Hillsdale, N.J.: The Analytic Press, 1996.

Gerson, R., S. Hoffman, M. Sauls, and D. Ulrici. "Family-of-Origin

Frames in Couples Therapy." *Journal of Marital and Family Therapy* 19, no. 4 (1993): 341–354.

Glenn, N. D. "Children of Divorce." *Psychology Today*, June 1985.

Gorski, Terence T. *Getting Love Right: Learning the Choices of Healthy Intimacy.* New York: Fireside, 1993.

Gotlib, Ian H., and William R. Avison. "Children at Risk for Psychopathology." In *Basic Issues in Psychopathology*, edited by Charles G. Costello, 271–314. New York: Gilford, 1993.

Gottman, John M. "Toward a Process Model of Men in Marriages and Families." In *Men in Families*, edited by A. Booth and A. C. Crouter. Mahwah, N.J.: Lawrence Erlbaum, 1998.

————. *Why Marriages Succeed or Fail . . . and How You Can Make Yours Last.* New York: Fireside, 1994.

Gottman, John M., and L. F. Katz. "Effects of Marital Discord on Young Children's Peer Interaction and Health." *Developmental Psychology* 25 (1989): 373–381.

Grych, John H. *Marital Conflict and Children's Adjustment: Initial Investigations of the Cognitive-Contextual Framework.* Doctoral dissertation, University of Illinois at Urbana-Champaign, 1991.

Grych, John H., and Frank D. Fincham. "Marital Conflict and Children's Adjustment: A Cognitive-Contextual Framework." *Psychological Bulletin* 108, no. 2 (1990): 267–290.

Guerin, Phillip J., and E. M. Gordon. "Trees, Triangles and Temperament in the Child-Centered Family." In *Evolving Models for Family Change: A Volume in Honor of Salvador Minuchin*, edited by H. C. Fishman and B. L. Rosman, 159–182. New York: Guilford, 1986.

Guttman, Herta A. "Children in Families with Emotionally Disturbed Parents." In *Children in Family Contexts: Perspectives on Treatment*, edited by Lee Combrinck-Graham, 252–276. New York: Guilford, 1989.

Hafner, R. Julian. *Marriage and Mental Illness: A Sex-Roles Perspective.* New York: Guilford, 1986.

Hampson, R. B., T. L. Hyman, and W. R. Beavers. "Age-of-Recall Effects on Family-of-Origin Ratings." *Journal of Marital and Family Therapy* 20, no. 1 (1994): 61–67.

Hare-Mustin, Rachel T. "Discourses in the Mirrored Room: A Postmodern Analysis of Therapy." *Family Process* 33 (1994):19–35.

Harkaway, Jill E. "Childhood Obesity: The Family Context." In *Children in Family Contexts: Perspectives on Treatment*, edited by Lee Combrinck-Graham, 231–251. New York: Guilford, 1989.

Harold, Gordon T., Frank D. Fincham, Lori N. Osborne, and Rand D. Conger. "Mom and Dad Are at It Again: Adolescent Perceptions of Marital Conflict and Adolescent Psychological Distress." *Developmental Psychology* 33, no. 2 (1997): 333–350.

Harter, Susan. "The Personal Self in Social Context." In *Self and Identity*, edited by Richard D. Ashmore and Lee Jussim, 81–105. New York: Oxford, 1997.

Heaton, Tim B., and Stan L. Albrecht. "Stable Unhappy Marriages." *Journal of Marriage and the Family* 53 (1991): 747–758.

Heller, Patrice E., and Beatrice Wood. "The Process of Intimacy: Similarity, Understanding and Gender." *Journal of Marital and Family Therapy* 24, no. 3 (1998): 273–288.

Hetherington, E. Mavis, and Kathleen M. Jodl. "Stepfamilies as Settings for Child Development." In *Stepfamilies: Who Benefits? Who Does Not?*, edited by A. Booth and J. Dunn, 55–79. Hillsdale, N.J.: Lawrence Erlbaum, 1994.

Hetherington, E. Mavis, M. Stanley-Hagan, and E. R. Anderson. "Marital Transitions: A Child's Perspective." *American Psychologist* 44 (1989): 303–312.

Holtzworth-Munroe, Amy, Stacia B. Beatty, and Kimberly Anglin. "The Assessment and Treatment of Marital Violence." In N. S. Jacobson and A. S. Gurman (eds.), *Clinical Handbook of Couple Therapy*, edited by N. S. Jacobson and A. S. Gurman, 317–339. New York: Guilford, 1995.

Hooven, Carole, John M. Gottman, and Lynn F. Katz. "Parental Meta-Emotion Structure Predicts Family and Child Outcomes." *Cognition and Emotion* 9, nos. 2 and 3 (1995): 229–264.

Howes, Paul, and Howard J. Markman. "Marital Quality and Child Functioning: Longitudinal Investigation." *Child Development* 60 (1989): 1044–1051.

Jekielek, S. M. "Parental Conflict, Marital Disruption and Children's Emotional Well-Being." *Social Forces* 76, no. 3 (1998), 905–936.

Josselson, Ruthellen. *Finding Herself: Pathways to Identity Development in Women.* New York: Jossey Bass, 1987.

————. *The Space Between Us.* New York: Sage, 1996.

Jurkovic, G. J. *Lost Childhoods: The Plight of the Parentified Child.* New York: Brunner/Mazel, 1997.

Katz, Lynn F. *Patterns of Marital Conflict and Children's Emotions.* Doctoral dissertation, University of Illinois at Urbana-Champaign, 1990.

Katz, Lynn F., and John M. Gottman. "Patterns of Marital Conflict Predict Children's Internalizing and Externalizing Behaviors." *Developmental Psychology* 29 (1993): 940–950.

Kelly, E. Lowell, and James J. Conley. "Personality and Compatibility: A Prospective Analysis of Marital Stability and Marital Satisfaction." *Journal of Personality and Social Psychology* 52, no. 1 (1987): 27–40.

Kelly, J. B. "Marital Conflict, Divorce and Children's Adjustment." *Child and Adolescent Psychiatric Clinics of North America* 7, no. 2 (1998): 259–271.

Kendall, Philip C., and Keith S. Dobson. "On the Nature of Cognition and Its Role in Psychopathology." In *Psycopathology and Cognition*, edited by Keith S. Dobson and Philip C. Kendall, New York: Academic Press, 1993.

Kerig, Patricia K. "Triangles in the Family Circle: Effects of Family Structure on Marriage, Parenting and Child Adjustment." *Journal of Family Psychology* 9, no. 1 (1995): 28–43.

Kerr, Michael, and Murray Bowen. *Family Evaluation.* New York: W. W. Norton, 1988.

Knudson-Martin, Carmen. "The Politics of Gender in Family Therapy." *Journal of Marital and Family Therapy* 23 (1997): 421–437.

Kohut, Heinz. "Thoughts on Narcissism and Narcissistic Rage." In *The Search for the Self*, edited by P. H. Orenstein, New York: International Universities Press, 1978.

Kozuch, Patricia, and Teresa M. Cooney. "Young Adults' Marital and

Family Attitudes: The Role of Recent Parental Divorce, and Family and Parental Conflict." *Journal of Divorce and Remarriage* 23 nos. 3 and 4 (1995): 45–62.

Krystal, H. *Integration and Self-Healing: Affect—Trauma—Alexithymia.* Hillsdale, N.J.: The Analytic Press, 1988.

Kulka, Richard A., and Helen Weingarten. "The Long-Term Effects of Parental Divorce in Childhood on Adult Adjustment." *Journal of Social Issues* 35, no. 4 (1979): 50–78.

Lachtar, Joan. *The Many Faces of Abuse.* Northvale, N.J.: Jason Aronson, 1998.

Langston, Donna. "Tired of Playing Monopoly?" In M. L. Anderson, *Race, Gender Class: An Anthology,* third edition, edited by M. L. Anderson and P. H. Collins, 126–136. Belmont, Calif.: Wadsworth, 1998.

Larson, Jeffrey H., Clark H. Hammond, and James M. Harper. "Perceived Equity and Intimacy in Marriage." *Journal of Marital and Family Therapy* 24 (1998): 487–506.

LaRossa, R. *Conflict and Power in Marriage.* Beverly Hills, Calif.: Sage, 1977.

Lee, Mo-Yee. "Trajectory of Influence of Parental Divorce on Children's Heterosexual relationships." *Journal of Divorce and Remarriage* 22, nos. 3 and 4 (1995): 55–76.

Lerner, Harriet. *The Dance of Anger: A Woman's Guide to Changing the Patterns of Intimate Relationships.* New York: Harper & Row, 1985.

———. *The Dance of Intimacy: A Woman's Guide to Courageous Acts of Change in Key Relationships.* New York: Harper & Row, 1989.

Levant, Ronald F. "Gender Equality and the New Psychology of Men: Comment on 'The Politics of Gender in Family Therapy.'" *Journal of Marital and Family Therapy* 23, no. 4 (1997): 439–444.

Lewis, Jerry M., and Margaret T. Owen. "Stability and Change in Family-of-Origin Recollections Over the First Four Years of Parenthood." *Family Process* 34, no. 4 (1995): 455–465.

Loewenstein, R. M. "Defensive Organization and Autonomous Ego Function." *Journal of the American Psychoanalytic Association* 15, no. 4 (1967): 795–809.

Mackey, Richard A., and Bernard A. O'Brien. *Lasting Marriages: Men and Women Growing Together.* Westport, Conn.: Praeger, 1995.

Margolin, Gayla. "Marital Conflict Is Not Marital Conflict Is Not Marital Conflict." In *Social Learning and Systems Approaches to Marriage and the Family,* edited by R. de V. Peters and R. J. McMahon, 193–216. New York: Brunner/Mazel, 1988.

McNeal, Cosandra, and Paul R. Amato. "Parents' Marital Violence: Long-Term Consequences for Children." *Journal of Family Issues* 19, no. 2 (1998): 123–139.

McQuillan, Julia, and Myra M. Ferree. "The Importance of Variation Among Men and the Benefits of Feminism for Families." In *Men in Families,* edited by Alan Booth and A. C. Crouter, 213–225. Mahwah, N.J.: Lawrence Erlbaum, 1998.

Meissner, W. W. "The Earliest Internalizations." In *Self and Object Constancy,* edited by Ruth F. Lax, Sheldon Bach, and J. Alexis Burland, 29–72. New York: Guilford, 1986.

Meyer, Shannon L., Christopher M. Murphy, Michele Cascardi, and Beverly Birns. "Gender and Relationships: Beyond the Peer Group." *American Psychologist* 46 (1991): 537.

Morrison, Helen L. *Children of Depressed Parents.* New York: Grune & Stratton, 1983.

Morrow, M. R. "The Influence of Dysfunctional Family Behaviors on Adolescent Career Exploration." *School Counselor* 42, no. 4 (1995): 311–316.

Moultrup, David J. *Husbands, Wives & Lovers.* New York: Guilford, 1990.

Neisser, Ulric. "Self-Narratives: True and False." In *The Remembering Self,* edited by Ulric Neisser and Robyn Rivush, 1–18. Cambridge, Mass.: The Press Syndicate of the University of Cambridge, 1994.

Neuman, M. Gary. "How Divorce Affects Kids." *Parents Magazine,* November 1998, 93.

Noller P. *Non Verbal Communication and Marital Interaction.* Pergamon Press, 1984.

O'Brien, Mary, Mudaita A. Bahadur, Christina Gee, Kathy Balto, and Stephanie Erber. "Child Exposure to Marital Conflict and Child

Coping Responses as Predictors of Child Adjustment." *Cognitive Therapy and Research* 21, no. 1 (1997): 39–59.

O'Leary, K. Daniel. "Marital Discord and Children: Problems, Strategies, Methodologies and Results." In *Children in Families Under Stress*, edited by A. Doyle, D. Gold, and D. Moskowitz, 35–46. San Francisco: Jossey Bass, 1984.

O'Leary, K. Daniel, and I. Arias. "Prevalence, Correlates and Development of Spouse Abuse." In *Social Learning and Systems Approaches to Marriage and the Family*, edited by R. de V. Peters and R. J. McMahon. New York: Brunner/Mazel, 1988.

Pollack, William. "Raising Loving Boys." *Working Mothers*, March 1999: 32–34.

———. *Real Boys*. New York: Random House, 1998.

Prince, S. E., and N. S. Jacobson. "A Review and Evaluation of Marital and Family Therapies for Affective Disorders." *Journal of Marriage and Family Therapy* 21 (1995): 377–401.

Prochaska, James, and Janice Prochaska. "Twentieth Century Trends in Marriage and Marital Therapy." In *Marriage and Marital Therapy*, edited by Thomas. J. Paolino and Barbara S. McCrady, 1–24. New York: Brunner/Mazel, 1978.

Rabin, Claire. *Equal Partners—Good Friends: Empowering Couples Through Therapy*. New York: Routledge, 1996.

Rausch, Harold L., W. A. Barry, R. K. Hertal, and M. A. Swain. *Communication, Conflict and Marriage*. San Francisco: Jossey-Bass, 1974.

Robins, Lee N., Sandra P. Schoenberg, Sandra J. Holmes, Kathryn S. Ratcliff, Alexandra Benham, and Jane Works. "Early Home Environment and Retrospective Recall: A Test for Concordance Between Siblings With and Without Psychiatric Disorders." *American Journal of Orthopsychiatry* 55 (1985): 27–41.

Rosen, Hugh. *Piagetian Dimensions of Clinical Relevance*. New York: Columbia University Press, 1985.

Sabatelli, Ronald M., and Stephen A. Anderson. "Family System Dynamics, Peer Relationships and Adolescents' Psychological Adjustment." *Family Relations* 40 (1991): 363–359.

Scanzoni, John, Karen Polonko, J. Teachman, and Linda Thompson. *The Sexual Bond.* New York: Sage, 1989.

Scarf, M. "Intimate Partners: Patterns in Love and Marriage." *Atlantic Monthly,* November 1986.

Scharff, David, and Jill Scharff. *Object Relations Family Therapy.* Northvale, N.J.: Jason Aronson, 1987.

Schneider, C. "The Struggle Towards a Feminist Practice in Family Therapy: Practice." In *Gender and Power in Families,* edited by Rosine J. Perelberg and Ann A. Miller, 118–134. New York: Tavistock, 1990.

Schwarz, J. Conrad, and David C. Zuroff. "Family Structure and Depression in Female College Students: Effects of Parental Conflict, Decision-Making Power and Inconsistency of Love." *Journal of Abnormal Psychology* 88, no. 4 (1979): 398–406.

Sheinberg, Marcia, and Peggy Penn. "Gender Dilemmas, Gender Questions and the Gender Mantra." *Journal of Marriage and Family Therapy* 17, no. 1 (1991): 33–44.

Siegel, Judith P. "Analysis of Projective Identification: An Object Relations Approach to Marital Treatment." *Journal of Clinical Social Work* 19 (1991): 71–81.

———. "Defensive Splitting in Couples." *Journal of Clinical Psychoanalysis,* 7, no. 3 (1998): 305–303.

———. "Destructive Conflict in Nonviolent Couples: A Treatment Guide." *Journal of Emotional Abuse* 1, no. 3 (1999): 65–85.

———. *Repairing Intimacy: An Object Relations Approach to Couples Therapy.* Northvale, N.J.: Jason Aronson, 1992.

Singer, Jerome L., and Peter Salovey. "Organized Knowledge Structures and Personality." In *Person, Schemas and Maladaptive Interpersonal Behaviors,* 33–79. Chicago: University of Chicago Press, 1991.

Snyder, Douglas K., and J. M. Velasquez. "Parental Influence on Gender and Marital Role Attitudes: Implications for Intervention." *Journal of Marital and Family Therapy* 23, no. 2 (1997): 191–201.

Spring, Janis A. *After the Affair: Healing the Pain and Rebuilding Trust When a Partner Has Been Unfaithful.* New York: HarperCollins, 1996.

Steil, Janice M. *Marital Equality: Its Relationship to the Well-Being of Husbands and Wives.* Thousand Oaks, Calif.: Sage, 1997.

Stierlin, H., and G. Weber. *Unlocking the Family Door: A Systemic Approach to the Understanding and Treatment of Anorexia Nervosa.* New York: Brunner/Mazel, 1989.

Stiver, Irene P. "The Meanings of 'Dependency' in Female-Male Relationships." In *Women's Growth in Connection: Writings from the Stone Center,* edited by J. V. Jordan, A. G. Kaplan, J. B. Miller, I. P. Stiver, and J. L. Surrey, 143–161. New York: Guilford, 1991.

Straussner, S. L. A. "The Impact of Alcohol and Other Drug Abuse on the American Family." *Drug and Alcohol Review* 13 (1994): 393–399.

Swidler, Ann. "Love and Adulthood in American Culture." In *Themes of Work and Love in Adulthood,* edited by N. Smelser and E. Erikson, Cambridge, Mass.: Harvard University Press, 1980.

Taffel, Ron, and Roberta Israeloff. *Why Parents Disagree and What You Can Do About It.* New York: Avon Books, 1995.

Thornton, A., and Deborah Freedman. "Changing Attitudes Toward Marriage and Single Life." *Family Planning Perspectives* 14, no. 6 (1982): 297–303.

Timmer, Susan G., Joseph Veroff, and Shirley Hatchett. "Family Ties and Marital Happiness: The Different Marital Experiences of Black and White Newlywed Couples." *Journal of Social and Personal Relationships* 13, no. 3 (1996): 335–359.

Turner, Martha. "Addictions in Marital/Relationship Therapy." In *Integrative Solutions,* edited by Gerald R. Weeks and Larry Hof, pp. 124–147. New York: Brunner/Mazel, 1995.

Wallerstein, Judith. "The Psychological Tasks of Marriage: Part 2." *American Journal of Orthopsychiatry* 66, no. 2 (1996): 217–227.

Wallerstein, Judith, and Sandra Blakeslee. *How and Why the Good Marriage Lasts.* New York: Houghton Mifflin, 1995.

———. *Second Chances: Men, Women and Children a Decade After Divorce.* New York: Ticknor & Fields, 1989.

Walters, Marianne, Betty Carter, Peggy Papp, and Olga Silverstein. *The Invisible Web: Gender Patterns in Family Relationships.* New York: Guilford, 1988.

Ward, Betty A. *Marital Quality, Marital Conflict—Tactics and Chil-*

dren's *Self-Image and School Behavior*. Doctoral dissertation, Yale University, 1988.

Waring, Edward M. "Marriages of Patients with Psychosomatic Illness." *General Hospital Psychiatry* 5 (1983): 49–53.

Waring, Edward M., Mary P. Tillman, L. Frelick, Lila Russell, and G. Weisz. "Concepts of Intimacy in the General Population." *Journal of Nervous and Mental Disease* 168, no. 8 (1980): 471–474.

Weeks, Gerald, and Larry Hof. "Commitment and Intimacy." In *Integrative Solutions*, edited by Gerald Weeks and Larry Hof. New York: Brunner/Mazel, 1995.

Wenning, Kenneth. *Men Are from Earth, Women Are from Earth*. Northvale, N.J.: Jason Aronson, 1998.

Westfall, April. "Extramarital Sex: The Treatment of the Couple." In *Treating Couples*, edited by Gerald R. Weeks, 163–190. New York: Brunner/Mazel, 1989.

———. "Working Through the Extramarital Trauma: An Exploration of Common Themes." In *Integrative Solutions*, edited by Gerald R. Weeks and Larry Hof. New York: Brunner/Mazel, 1995.

Whitbourne, Susan K., and Joyce B. Ebmeyer. *Identity and Intimacy in Marriage: A Study of Couples*. New York: Springer-Verlag, 1990.

White, L. K., and A. Booth. "The Transition to Parenthood and Marital Quality." *Journal of Family Issues* 6, no. 4 (1985): 435–449.

Whitehead, Tony L., and Barbara V. Reid. *Gender Constructs and Social Issues*. Urbana: University of Illinois Press, 1992.

Whiteside, Mary F. "The Parental Alliance Following Divorce: An Overview." *Journal of Marital and Family Therapy* 24, no. 1 (1998): 3–24.

Worden, Mark, and Barbara Worden. *The Gender Dance in Couples Therapy*. Pacific Grove, Calif.: Brooks/Cole, 1998.

Wynne, Lyman C., and Adele R. Wynne. "The Quest for Intimacy." *Journal of Marital and Family Therapy* 12 (1986): 383–394.

Zeanah, Charles H., Neil W. Boris, and Julie A. Larrieu. "Infant Development and Developmental Risk: A Review of the Past 10 Years." *Journal of the American Acadamy of Child & Adolescent Psychiatry* 36, no. 2 (1997): 165–178.

Index

Abuse
  children witness to, 140–41
  emotional, 94–96
  narcissistically vulnerable parent
    and, 95–96
  physical and threat of physical,
    134, 140, 158
  power in relationship, 132–34
  psychological impact on child, 140
  repeat of abusive patterns in next
    generation's relationships, 141
  spousal, 140
  verbal, 14, 82, 134, 158–59
Acting out behaviors
  marital tension/conflict and, 38,
    141

  recreating parents' negative behav-
    ior with peers, 11, 141
Adolescent children
  anorexia in, 24
  anxiety, 42, 142–43
  depression, 42
  emotional separation from parents,
    20
  perception of family, 5
  suicide attempt, example (Helen),
    151–52
  withdrawal, example, (Ben), 49–52
Affairs, extramarital
  birth of child and, 36
  child discovers, 102–3
  consequences of, 100–1

Affairs, extramarital (*cont.*)
  effect on children, 101–3
  effect on grown children, 104–5
  example, child's discovery of affair
    (Glenn family), 103–4
  example, conflict avoidance
    (Howard and Penny), 124–26
  example, defensive posture of
    grown child in relationship (Kirt
    and Sandra), 105–8
  prevalence, among men, 100
  saving marriage after, 108
  violation of trust and, 85
Affection, xvii, 166–67
  lack of, sign of troubled marriage,
    166
  positive modeling and children, 14
African American female-headed
    households, 110
Age-related perceptions, 4, 5
Aggressive behavior, 12, 134, 141,
    145
Alcoholic families, 13
  ACOA (adult children of alco-
    holics), 121–23
  "identified problem person," 122
  parentified child in, 54–56
  roles of children, 13
Anger
  avoidance and fear of, 120, 159
  balancing with love and humor,
    163
  children's, 14, 102
  demands of others on marriage
    partners and, 19
  disagreeing without, 136
  masking uncomfortable feelings,
    182

in men, and vulnerability, 46, 50
  stuffing feelings, 13, 133, 150
Anxiety
  adolescent, 42
  conflict in family and, 142–43
  enmeshed families, 123
  in family life, effect on children, 13
  gender-determined roles and, 45
Appreciation, demonstrating,
    170–72
Attention deficit disorder (ADD), 28

Bandura, Alfred, 2–3
Barnes, Gill, 30–31
Bernstein, Ann, 5
Bickering, 98–99
Birth of child and stress on marriage,
    34–37
  revival of painful memories in fam-
    ilies of origin, 39
Blame (blaming)
  behavior parent-to-parent, 14–15,
    120
  children blaming themselves, 5, 161
  narcissistically vulnerable parent,
    95
  trigger areas for children and, 15
Blended families. *See* Stepfamilies
Brown, Emily, 101, 102
Building a better marriage, 180–97
  accountability and forgiveness,
    194–95
  example of change (Helen), 185–86
  gender-based assumptions, chang-
    ing, 186–87
  imagining outcomes of change,
    180–81
  importance to child, 195–96

openness to change, example
(Richard and Molly), 187–92
questions, 197
self-awareness and, 181–83
separate past from present, 193–94
tacit beliefs and expectations,
183–84
team, operating as a, 192–93

Child-centered families, 34–36,
39–42
parenting as an escape (example,
Lynn and Mark), 39–41
problems for children, 41–42
Children
age-related perceptions, 4, 5
beliefs about intimacy and future
relationships, xv, xvii, 1
conflict, effects on child, *see* Conflict and long-term effects
emotions acknowledged and
responded to, 52–53
fantasy, and coloring of beliefs,
10–11
focus of parental re-directed anger,
14
"here and now" reactions, xvii
identification with parents, 8–10,
68, 71
internalized couple, 10–11
learning through imitation and
observation, 1–2, 3
looped in parental conflicts, 15,
116, 126–29, 145–46, 160
mental road map (schema), 4–5, 6,
166
parent's emotions centered on
instead of spouse, 53–54

perceptions thought beyond their
awareness, xv, xvi, 2, 3
recreation of parents' marriage, xiv,
11
security, need for, 101, 166
troubled, *see* Troubled children
unique sensibilities among siblings,
6–7
Communication
example (Richard and Molly),
188–92
open-mindedness and, 173, 187
reactive responses, 154, 193
reactive responses, example (Gail
and Mario), 174–76
Conflict and long-term effects of,
xvii, 139–64. *See also* Negotiating differences; Violence
abuse of power in relationship,
132–34
avoidance, problems created by,
116, 159
child suicide attempt and, example
(Helen), 151–52
children as detours, 152–53
children looped in parental conflicts, 15, 116, 126–29, 145–46,
160
children as peacemakers, 150–51,
153
"cold wars," 144–45
divorce, consequences of, 145–446
do's and don'ts for parents, 158–63,
195
fighting through the children,
example (Stanton family),
148–50
fights about children, 146–48

Conflict and long-term effects of (*cont.*)
  financial pressures, example (Peter
    and Catherine), 154–57
  grown child, problems that surface,
    153–54
  in home, 12–13
  hyperactivity in child and, exam-
    ple (Jordan), 143–44
  narcissistically vulnerable people
    and problems, 95
  questions, 164
  walking out, 134
Cowan, Phillip and Carolyn, 38–39,
  122
Criticism
  parent to parent, 14
  parent to child, 155

Dating
  choice of partner, 13
  divorce and inability to trust/test-
    ing behaviors, 109, 154
  emotional issues emerge, 13
  example, daughter with disre-
    spected mother (Susan), 70–72
  high-conflict homes and grown
    children, 144–45
  parent's affair and inability to trust
    partner, 105
Daughters
  disrespected father and, 79
  disrespected father and, example
    (Rose and Marvin), 80–81
  disrespected mother and, 69
  disrespected mother, example
    (Susan), 70–72
  exposure to physical violence, 141

-father relationship, example
    (Helen), 184–86
  mother's depression, example
    (Hanzel family), 127–29
  siding with mother against father,
    145, 184
Death of parent, 57, 58–59
Defensive postures, negative identification with parent and, 9–10
Dependency, 13
  gender-determined roles and,
    44–47
  high-conflict homes and, 144
  importance of in relationship,
    47–48
  loss of parent in childhood and, 57
  reciprocity (mutual caretaking
    and) and example of Steven
    Lewis, 61–64
Depression
  adolescent, 42
  children's, 14, 141, 144
  gender-determined roles and, 45
  love relationship and, 19
  mitigation of, 42
  mother's, 142, 149
  mother's, example (Hanzel family),
    127–29
Disrespect between parents, damaging effect of, 68–69, 195
Divorce, 108–13
  absent parent after, and emotional
    devastation of child, 109,
    111–12
  affairs and, 105
  child's birth as cause of, 35
  effects on grown children, 109–11

high-conflict homes versus, 145–46
minimizing damage to child, 111–13
rate in U.S., 18
relationship with "ex," xviii–xix
sleeper effect, 153–54
trust issues and, 85
Duchenne's disease, 62–63

Eating disorders, 24
Ebmeyer, Joyce, 53
Emotions
acknowledging and responding to children's, 52–53, 116
affective power (hysteria or emotional outbursts to manipulate events), 133
belittled or ridiculed, 51
"coaching," 53
deflected in addictions or health problems, 46
dependency and vulnerability in successful relationship, 20–21, 188–92
fear of and resulting deflection, ignoring, or release, 116–17, 121, 133
gender roles and expression of, 147–48
men and acknowledgement of, 48
paying attention to, 82
reactivity, passed from generation to generation, 14
self-awareness of, 181–82
"stuffing," 13, 133, 150
submerged, 13

trust between partners and, 85–86
violence and denial of feelings, 89
vulnerability in children, 14
Enmeshed families, 21–28
conflict and anxiety in children, 123
cross-generational ties, example (Perlmutter family), 25–28
entitlement and example (Paul and Irene), 23–24
loyalties and, 22–23
problems for children, 24–28
Environment (family)
alcoholism in, 13
anxiety in, 13
conflict in, 12–13, 139–64
effect on children, 2, 14
flexible, 176–77
secure, positive effect, 14, 101, 166
stress in, 25–28
warm, relaxed, playful, 178

Family
balance between self and others, 20–21
child-centered, 34–36
childhood family of partner impinges on, 20–21
enmeshed, 21–28, 123
parenting as an escape, 39–41
secrets, 55, 97, 103
single parent, effect on children, 110
workaholic, 30–34
Family therapy. *See also specific examples of couples*
intercultural couples, 136

Family therapy (*cont.*)
  neglects to consider client's par
    ents' relationship, xv
Father
  absent after divorce, 111–12
  affairs and son as confidant, 103
  conflict with adolescent son, exam
    ple (Randi and Adam), 117–21
  -daughter relationship, example
    (Helen), 184–86
  disrespected and daughters, 79
  disrespected and daughters, exam
    ple (Rose and Marvin), 80–81
  disrespected and sons, 76–77
  disrespected and sons, example
    (Tom and Patricia), 77–79
  emotional connection with wife
    and emotional availability to
    children, 48–49
  marital conflict and behavior
    toward child, 142
  reactive to feminine qualities in
    sons, 147
  -son relationships, 48–49, 147
  workaholic (Sampson family
    example), 32–34
Fears of abandonment or feeling left
  alone, 13, 109, 112
Financial issues, 130–31
  explosive issue, example (Peter and
    Catherine), 154–57
  "Junior/Senior Partner," 131
  prenuptial agreements, example
    (Robin and Sam), 86–91
  trust and, 85, 86, 98
Forgiveness, 177–78
  using power of to improve mar
    riage, 194–95

Freud, Sigmund, 77
Friendship between spouses, example
  (Alan and Megan), 167–70

Gorski, Terrence, 121
Gottman, Jon, 145, 165

Harkaway, Jill, 24
"Hot buttons," 14
Hyperactivity, 143–44

Identification, 8–10
  disidentification, 9, 77, 110, 133, 186
  emotional vulnerability, 9
  modeling both parents, 8–9
  respect and, 68, 71
Infidelity. *See* Affairs, extramarital
Insecurity, 13, 141, 144
Intercultural couples, 136
Internalized couple, 10–11
Intimacy
  factors for development of, 29
  independence versus interdepen
    dence and, 45
  predictable problems of daughter
    with disrespected mother, 69
  trust as necessary ingredient, 84–85

Jekyll/Hyde aspect of troubled chil
  dren, 12
Josselson, Ruthellen, 9, 29
Judgmental behavior, 15
Jurkovic, Gregory, 153

Kohut, Heinz, 67

Lies
  alcoholic family, 122

children involved by parent in, 97–98

deceitful behaviors and, 97

Loyalty, divided or tested, 14, 101

child asked to take sides, 160

parent attempts to turn children against spouse, 101

Mackey, Richard, 48

Marriage. *See also specific aspects/conflicts*

affection, xvii, 166–67

building a better, 180–97

conflict resolution, xvii

happy, study of, 48

friendship in, example (Alan and Megan), 167–70

historic expectations and, 29

laughter as key ingredient, 172

lifelong influence of, 16

negotiation, xvii, 115–38

post-modern, 36

priority of, xvii, 18–43, 168

respect, xvii, 67–83

roller-coaster, 95–96, 124

schema of, positive and negative, 14, 15–17, 20, 166, 193–94

seven key ingredients, xvii

support and mutual caring, xvii, 44–67

traditional, and power issues, 130–31

trust, xvii, 57, 84–114

unhappy, 18–19

Men

affection and acknowledgement of feelings, 48

anger in, 46

caretaker role, and superiority, 72, 73–76

caring, demonstrations of, versus women, 47

feelings of vulnerability, inability to acknowledge, 45, 46, 188–92

independence and intimacy problems, 45–52

learned behavior and gender roles, 45–47, 146–47, 187

power and gender roles, 129–30

Mothers

balancing roles of wife and mother, 37

children as confidant of, 27–28

depression, example (Hanzel family), 127–29

disrespected and daughter, 69

disrespected and daughter, example (Susan), 70–72

excessive loyalty to and example (Sampson family), 32–34, 37–37

excessive over-involvement with childhood family, 24, 26

identity dependent on child, 28

marital conflict and behavior toward child, 142

-son relationships, 147–48

working, 30–31, 35–36

Narcissistically vulnerable parents, 94–96

Negotiating differences, xvii, 115–38

example, controlling husband, depressed wife, child becomes assertive (Hanzel family), 127–29

Negotiating differences (*cont.*)
  example, different expectations for
    the children (Adam and Randi),
    117–21
  fear of feelings and, 116–17
  inability to see differences, exam-
    ple (Howard and Penny),
    124–26
  marriages of the children of alco-
    holics (ACOA), 121–23
  overly dependent (enmeshed) fam-
    ilies, 123
  pathological power, 132–34
  power, 129–32
  power, negotiating, 135
  questions, 138
  speaking through the children, 126
  talking face-to-face, 136–37
Nervousness, 143
Nightmares, 40, 41

Obese or overweight children, 11, 24
O'Brien, Bernard, 48
Oedipal complex and disrespected
  father, 77
Overreaction
  communication and reactive
    responses, 154, 193
  gender roles and reactive fathers,
    147–48
  negative identification with parent
    and, 9–10, 71

Parentified child, 54–61
  adult consequences, 56–57
  in alcoholic family (McNeil family
    example), 54–56
  conflict and, 153

example of adult in relationship
  (Irene and Bob), 57–61
  maternal abuse and, 141
Partner, choice of, and recreation of
  parents' marriage, xv, xvii, 13, 141
"Perfect" children or super-responsi-
  ble, 13, 55, 96, 141
Piaget, Jean, 4–5
Positives, emphasizing, 165–79
  appreciation, 170–72
  change, willingness to, 178
  flexibility, 176–77
  forgiveness, 177–78
  friendship, 167–70
  laughter, 172–73
  open-mindedness, 173–76
  physical affection, 166–67
  questions, 178
  ratio of positive negative, optimal,
    165
  warm, relaxed family atmosphere,
    178
Power issues, 129–37
  angry, controlling parent, 119–20
  children as pawns, 99
  emotional manipulation, 133
  example, (Klein family), 99–100
  finances, 130–31
  gender roles and, 129–30
  outsider influence, 132–33
  pathological (abuse), 132–34
  traditional marriage, 130
  walking out, 134
  withholding resources, 134
Prenuptial agreements, example
  Robin and Sam, 86–91
Preschool children
  behavioral/emotional problems, 41

competition between parents and
  toddler behavior, 38
conflict, reaction to, 143, 144
example, hyperactivity in response
  to conflict (Jordan), 143–44
perception of family, 5
Priority of marriage, xvii, 18–43, 168
  birth of child and changes in rela-
    tionship, 36–38, 140
  child-centered families, 34–36
  emotional unavailability and prob-
    lems for children, 41–42
  enmeshed families, 21
  family connectedness, stages of,
    20–21
  parenting as an escape, 39–41
  primacy of partner over others,
    29–30
  problems for children and parent-
    grown children involvement,
    24–28, 41–42
  questions, 43
  revival of unhappy marriages,
    38–39
  workaholic families, 30–34
"Private reality," 7

Respect, xvii, 67–83
  daughters and disrespected fathers,
    79–81
  daughters and disrespected moth-
    ers, 69–72
  greatest harm to children from dis-
    respect, 82
  positive modeling and children,
    14, 68
  questions, 83
  self-esteem and, 67–69, 81–82

sons and disrespected fathers,
  76–79
sons and disrespected mothers,
  72–76
troubled child and, 81–82
Roller-coaster marriage, 95–96, 124
  example (Howard and Penny),
    124–26

Scanzoni, John, 131
Scharff, David and Jill, 10
Schema, 4–5
  changing, 6
  memories and, 6
  positive of marriage, 14, 15–17, 20
  power of, 6
  separating past from present,
    193–94
  as "tacit knowledge," 7–8, 183–86
School
  achievement and emotional coach-
    ing, 53
  adjustment problems, 38
  inability to concentrate, 141
School-age children
  competition between parents and
    adjustment of, 38
  difficulty in maintaining friend-
    ships, 42
  perception of family, 5
Self-esteem, 14, 55, 81–82, 134, 153
  cornerstone of mental health,
    67–69
  parentified child, 153
  low, in child, 14, 55, 81–82, 134,
    153
Selfishness/self-centered behaviors,
  64–65

Sex in relationships
 children confided in, 161–62
 infidelity and emotional exclusivity, 100–8
 infrequent, 50, 73
 problems in, 40–41
Shyness, 11, 40
Siblings
 differing memories between, 6–7
 "private reality," 7
Social learning, 2–3
Sons
 disrespected father and, 76–77
 disrespected father and example
  (Tom and Patricia), 77–79
 disrespected mother and, 72–73
 disrespected mother and example
  (Roy and Jan), 73–76
 exposure to physical violence, 141
 -father relationships, 48–49
 father's infidelity and attitude
  toward women, 103
 gender roles and reactive fathers,
  147–48
 parents with different expectations
  for, example (Randi and Adam),
  117–21
 siding with father against mother,
  145–46, 184
Stepfamilies, 5
 conflicting loyalties, 85
 example, defensive posture of stepparent (Kirt and Sandra), 105–8
 example, financial and trust issues
  (Robin and Sam), 86–91
 example (Roy and Jan), 73–76
 resentment of children toward new

parent, example (Frank family),
 91–94
Stress, in children of enmeshed families, 25–28
Suicide attempts, 151–52
Supportive behavior of parents
 (interdependence), 15–17,
 44–66
 child of alcoholic father (McNeil
  family), 54–56
 children as emotional anchor,
  53–54
 emotional availability to children,
  52–53
 example of couple (Paul and
  Elaine), 49–52
 independence and gender-determined roles, 45–52
 lack of support and consequences,
  64–65
 parentified child, as adult, 56–57
 parentified child, example in relationship (Irene and Bob), 57–61
 reciprocity, 61–62
 reciprocity, example of couple with
  sick child, 62–64
Symptoms of troubled children, 11,
 12, 13, 15, 24–28, 55, 96
 ADD, 28, 143
 aggression, 122, 134, 141, 145
 anger, 14, 56
 anxiety, 42, 142–43
 causes (non-physical), xiv, 11–15,
  24–25, 41–42, 94–96, 152–53
 children of alcoholics, 13, 121–23
 delayed until dating and marriage,
  15

dependency, 144

depression, 14, 42, 141, 144

difficulty in maintaining friendships, 42

disruptive behavior to stop parents'
conflict, 12, 28, 152

fears of abandonment, 13

insecurity, 141, 144

nightmares, 40, 41

quiet/overly restrained/"perfect,"
13, 55, 96, 141

school-related, 38, 122, 141

self-esteem low, 14, 55, 81–82,
134, 153

shyness, 11, 40

"stuffing" feelings, 13, 133, 150

substance abuse, 143

"Tacit knowledge," 7–8, 183–84
example of father-daughter relationship (Helen), 184–86
gender-based assumptions, 186–87
Taffel, Ron, 35
Tension, negative identification with
parent and, 9–10, 71
Toronto's Hospital for Sick Children,
xiv, 62
Troubled children, 11–15. *See also*
Symptoms of troubled children
children of alcoholics, roles, 13
children of ACOA parents, 122
children of hysterical or emotionally distraught parents, 133
children of narcissistically vulnerable parent, 96
disrespect in family and, 81–82
problem child, 12, 13

Trust, 84–114
alcoholic family, 122
blended families and example
(Frank family), 91–94
commitment to each other's well-
being, 85
commitment to sexual and emotional exclusivity, and examples,
100–108
divorce and, 108–13
emotional abuse, 94–96
emotional wariness and dependency issues, 57
intimacy requirement, 84
lack of, 11
lies and violation of, 97–98
marriage and children's ability to,
xvii, 14
prenuptial agreement and example
Robin and Sam, 86–91
questions, 114
violation of a partner's needs and
example (Klein family), 98–100

Unfinished business, internalized
from parents' marriage, 11

Violence in families
alcoholic families, 122
children as peacemakers, 150–52
denial of feelings and, 89
severe psychological damage to
child, 140, 158
threat of, 134

Wallerstein, Judith, 105, 141, 153–54
Whitbourne, Susan, 53

Women
  assertiveness, problems with,
    46–47
  caring, demonstrations of, versus
    men, 47
  conflict avoidance, 46, 159
  emotional deprivation from hus-
    band, 53–54

  issues of support and dependency
    in relationship, 45–46
  learned behavior and gender roles,
    45–47, 146, 187
  power and gender roles, 129–30
Workaholic families, 30–34